Sunset

Home Offices
& Workspaces

By the
Editors of
Sunset Books
and
Sunset Magazine

Updated rolltop desk, also shown on page 69.

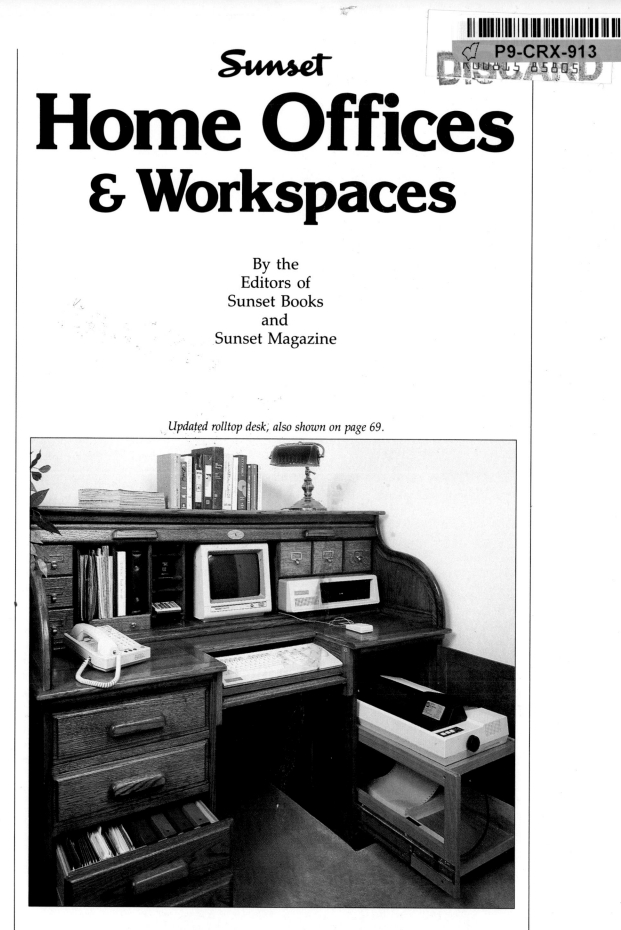

Lane Publishing Co. ■ Menlo Park, California

High-style files, also shown on page 75.

Developmental Editor
Helen Sweetland

Coordinating Editor
Linda J. Selden

Contributing Editors
Susan Warton
Geoff Alexander
Don Vandervort

Design
Joe di Chiarro

Illustrations
Bill Oetinger
Rik Olson
Mark Pechenik

Photo Stylist
JoAnn Masaoka

Photographers: Clyde Childress, 26; **Stephen Marley,** 13 top, 29; **Jack McDowell,** 27, 28 bottom, 30 left, 31 left, 70 top, 72 bottom, 80; **Rob Super,** 15, 71 top; **Darrow M. Watt,** 30 right; **Tom Wyatt,** 1, 2, 5–12, 13 bottom, 14, 16–25, 28 top, 31 right, 32, 65–69, 70 bottom, 71 bottom, 72 top, 73–79.

Cover: With modular office furniture, you can custom design a work center for virtually any space. Office furniture by Techline, Inc. Location courtesy of By Design. Cover design by Liz Ross. Photography by Tom Wyatt.

Editor, Sunset Books: Elizabeth L. Hogan

Second printing June 1989

Working at home

The home work force has expanded in recent years to include a broad sector of the population—from salespeople to computer programmers, volunteers to freelance illustrators. If you work at home, this book will supply the inspiration, design ideas, and practical data you'll need to plan an efficient and comfortable home office. From ergonomic principles to advice on choosing the right floor covering, all the details are here—plus plentiful artwork and color photography. We've even included step-by-step instructions for office furnishings you can make yourself.

Many people assisted us in gathering and checking the material for this book. We are especially grateful to Dave Alpert of The Ratcliff Architects; Louise Bragato of The Computer Furniture Company; Rebecca Burger-Barson of Lindsay's; Kathleen D. Jacobus and Patti A. Neer of Ambiance Associates; Susan Knight of Interior Design Works, Ltd.; Steve and Joan Osburn; Dean Santner; Paula P. Wildanger of Eurodesign, Ltd.; and Judd Williams of Williams & Foltz.

We also extend special thanks to Frances Feldman for editing the manuscript, to Joan Erickson for researching the office planning information, and to Liz Ross for scouting locations for some of our photographs.

Contents

Artist's flat files, also shown on page 74.

Finding a Space to Work

Unless you live in a grand house, where parlors and studies abound and bedrooms open onto private sitting rooms, finding space for a home office may seem like quite a challenge. Actually, though, potential office space is almost always lurking in plain view. Finding it simply requires a shift of perspective, which this chapter can help you achieve.

Unless you're fortunate enough to have a spare room, the most common way to squeeze in a home office is to borrow space from an existing room—diplomatically, so as not to disturb the room's original purpose. That's why we begin this chapter with home offices that share space with a guest room, family room, or kitchen. Depending on the nature of your work, you may well be able to adapt some of the space-sharing ideas shown in the photos.

Perhaps you'd like the luxury of being able to spread out in a detached studio or remodeled attic, basement, or garage. With careful planning, you can transform one of these spaces into a comfortable office that's spacious enough to accommodate both you and your clients.

If you don't need quite so much room, consider the little nooks and crannies that abound in just about every home. Hallways, staircase landings, and under-the-stairway areas offer possibilities for office space. So do closets; even a small one can usually be fitted with a desk and shelves. With proper lighting and ventilation, it can provide a cozy, compact workspace that's quiet and private.

You may be surprised, and perhaps reassured, when you see in the color photography that follows many examples of tight spaces that are designed for both comfort and maximum office use. Remember that the right furnishings—along with an efficient office layout—can make the difference between cramped and shipshape quarters.

Capitalize *on a convenient corner to create office space. Here, cabinetwork turns part of a guest bedroom into a family computer center. Interior design: Lynn Williams of The French Connection.*

Part-time Positions

SHARING A GUEST ROOM

Growth Potential

Now you see it, but sometimes you don't. Built into the wall system shown below are work surfaces that slide out like bread boards, as well as a desk that folds down to reveal a cozily closeted computer. Like the Murphy bed on the room's opposite wall, each device shuts away out of sight when not needed. Interior design: Legallet-Trinkner Design Associates. Furniture design: Eurodesign, Ltd.

...part-time positions

Wrapped in Cabinetry

Built-in cabinets, counters, and shelves tailor a small room to dual purpose as a family computer center and guest sleeping quarters. Finely worked details include the corner desk area, a bookcase alcove, and pull-out shelves flanking the sofa bed. Interior design: Lynn Williams of The French Connection.

...part-time positions

On the Move

Since most of the furniture in this office rolls around on casters, it can be wheeled out of the way when the sofa bed is needed for overnight guests. Besides moving when you nudge it, the drafting table has an additional swing-up work surface; it also stores supplies in its commodious base. Furniture design: Barbara R. Wolfe and Osburn Design.

Sharing the Family Room

COMPUTER QUARTERS

Secret Compartments

Sharing one end of the family room with a traditional writing desk, polished cabinetry conceals a complete computer work center. The keyboard slides out on its own shelf; the printer emerges from a deep, open-sided drawer. Furniture design: Interior Design Works, Ltd.

Borrowing from the Kitchen

COOKS' COMMAND
CENTERS

Tucked Away

Around the corner from spills, steam, and other kitchen hazards, this built-in desk offers the cook a quiet retreat. Its rolltop cover allows quick concealment of interrupted paperwork. Architect: Robert C. Peterson.

Clearinghouse

Unscrambling a calendar, talking on the phone, planning a menu, or penning a thank-you—all these tasks become easier to expedite from a kitchen desk like this one. Interior design: Barbara Jacobs.

...borrowing from the kitchen

Businesslike Buffet

Sometimes you're in the kitchen to peel potatoes, other times to access data. Shifting its function along with its height, this kitchen counter can accommodate either enterprise. Design: Marilyn Woods and Brian Grossi.

Administrative Post

Meticulous management of a busy household starts with this carefully planned kitchen office. A smooth continuation of the room's other cabinetwork, the desk area includes a much-used lateral file (shown open at left). Architect: W. L. McElhinney.

Pots, Pans & Poetry

Flowing flawlessly with the clean design of its kitchen surroundings, this compact office space is designed for easy accessibility when you'd rather produce metaphors than meals. Architect: Gilbert Oliver.

Sphere of Influence

Set unobtrusively into the passageway leading from the kitchen to the dining room, this small but efficient office remains separate, even while sharing one large space. Architect: Obie Bowman.

Detached from the House

FOR PRIVACY, QUIET

Friendly First Impression

Occupying its own spacious, separate studio, this attorney's office gains warmth from a wood-burning stove and garden views through a large triangular window. Furniture design: Williams & Foltz.

Cottage Industry

Draped in flowering vines, this two-story cottage houses an interior designer's office and showroom, along with a kitchen and garage. Downstairs, the furnishings welcome clients; a more private office is maintained in the loft above. Interior design: Rela's Homework.

Upward
Mobility

ENTERPRISING ATTICS

High Style

As it interfaces with high-tech equipment, this two-sided, custom-designed unit also interprets its attic location. Steps on one side echo the steeply angled ceiling, turning inconvenience into visual interest. Furniture design: Limn.

…upward mobility

Skylit Aerie

A boldly gabled ceiling and floods of natural light infuse this attic with an airy clarity. Door (shown at right) opens to a small balcony and exterior staircase. Skylights, supplemented by industrial lamps, allow an illumination possible only in spaces lodged directly under the roof. Architect: Alan Dreyfuss.

Above It All

Windows surround this studio with restful views, bathe it in natural light, and cool it by cross ventilation. At the center of the spacious floor, wire storage cubes divide the work area (shown below) from the conference table.

...upward mobility

Lofty Status
The bold rooflines of this architectural office emphasize its lofty status in the treetops.
Dramatic windows surround work areas with woodland views. Architect: Edmund Berger.

Down to Basics

BASEMENT BUSINESSES

Shapely Shelving
Built to conceal pipes, wedge over desk also opens up intriguing storage niches. Triangular theme continues, on a smaller scale, down side of bookcase. Recessed lights can be removed for access to plumbing and electrical systems. Design: Osburn Design.

Twice as Big
One of the biggest spaces in most homes—and conveniently out of the way—a basement can open up new horizons for a shared office or studio. Design: Osburn Design.

...down to basics

Low Overhead

Bright white and natural wood trim lend a professional image of energy and efficiency to this office space. L-shaped work center at right looks out on a garden path that flanks the basement wall. Reception area, above, opens onto its own patio. Interior design: Gail Woolaway & Associates.

Garage
Conversions

SPACE TO SPREAD OUT

Garage Getaway

For people who work to relax, this roomy converted garage provides ample work surfaces and storage for craft projects, as well as a brightly lit window seat that offers an inviting retreat. The friendly Dutch door allows contact with the family, while also discouraging intrusion. Design: Sylvia Reay.

A Creative Solution

When a wall of glass replaced the old swing-up door, this garage became a solar-heated office. Dark tile laid on the garage slab absorbs excess heat; mini-blinds control both natural lighting and solar gain. Solar design: David R. Roberts of Dr. Solar.

Closet Industries

HIDDEN OFFICE SPACE

What once flourished as a bedroom closet now pursues a second career as a computer work center and pocket-size library. High-tech equipment looks user-friendly in comfortable, old-fashioned surroundings.

Take-over

An expendable closet, minus its doors, becomes a trim and tidy home office, without intruding upon the family room in which it's located. The closet's width easily embraces a desk. Ledgers support wide shelves, tracks and brackets hold shorter ones.

An Economic Study

Careful economy of space keeps everything within easy reach for research and writing in this converted closet. The desktop area is illuminated by a long fluorescent fixture; overhead lights add a softer incandescent wash. When not in use, the study disappears behind folding doors. Architect: David Jeremiah Hurley.

Pocket-size Offices

SQUEEZING IN A DESK

Under the Stairs
A bifold door closes up this under-the-stairway office when it's not in use. Opened, the angled door partially screens the work area, affording extra privacy. Architect: George Cody. Associate: William Smart.

Upper Echelon
A mere snippet of space stolen from the upstairs landing, this home office perches high above the household below. An overhead skylight illuminates the work area. Architect: Robert C. Peterson.

Cut to Measure

Tailored to fit an oddly angled alcove off the master bedroom, this office makes maximum use of every inch. Along with storage space for books and oversize papers, it manages comfortable leg room, as well. Architect: David Jeremiah Hurley. Interior design: Jois.

Hidden Asset

Adding handsome oak shelving and a desk to this chimney section transforms a previously wasted corner into a much-used and valuable asset. Design: Tom Keller.

Planning Your Office

The plan you devise for your home office will be as individual as the work you do there. Whether your home workspace is the setting for a small business or simply a quiet spot for cataloging stamps, designing a quilt, or writing a novel, you'll need to plan it carefully if it's to serve you well.

Zoning restrictions. If you plan to operate a business from your home, you'll need to know the local zoning ordinances that govern home occupations. In some areas, the use of detached buildings, separate office entrances, and even signs is prohibited. Some counties and municipalities also limit the amount of a home's square footage that can be devoted to a business. In many cases, you cannot store goods in your home or make any retail transactions there.

Note, too, that many localities prohibit home businesses that generate traffic, parking demand, or deliveries greater than that customarily associated with a residence. Often, no one but the legal occupants can be employed on the site in connection with a home business.

Zoning regulations for home occupations vary greatly from one area to another, so be sure to check your local requirements.

The planning process. This chapter is designed to guide you through the entire process of planning your home office, from choosing equipment to applying the finishing touches.

We begin by describing some basic office machines and furniture—from disk drives and computer printers to desk chairs and lamps. Because some of these items are expensive, one-time purchases, you'll want to make your decisions carefully. To help you choose the right furnishings, we offer a special eight-page, illustrated guide.

Once you decide on the equipment and furniture your office will need, we'll help you examine your home from top to bottom to find just the right workspace location. Virtually every home has potential office space in the form of a spare room; a portion of an existing room (such as a bedroom or family room); a garage, attic, or basement; or a closet or other pocket-size area.

Developing an office layout that takes into account the way you want to work, the equipment you need, and the space you have available will ensure that your workspace is comfortable and efficient. Following our step-by-step instructions, you'll learn how to draw accurate floor plans and elevations, as well as how to experiment with layouts, using scale cutouts of furniture.

Then we'll help you plan the finishing touches, including both task and ambient lighting and coverings for floors, walls, and windows. These details not only add to your comfort but also help determine the overall look of your workspace.

Though only you can decide which chair is most comfortable or what kind of storage your work requires, you may need to turn to a professional for design advice or remodeling work. Guidelines for choosing and working with professionals appear on pages 62–63.

Thanks to computers, *organizing office space today presents a challenge; success relies on careful planning and execution. Furniture design: Eurodesign, Ltd.*

Getting Equipped

An efficient and comfortable home office doesn't just happen—it's the result of careful planning. Determining your equipment and furniture needs in the beginning will help you decide how large a workspace you'll need and how that workspace can best be laid out.

Like new cars, office equipment comes in a diversity of makes and models, with a wide assortment of optional features. For this reason, it's important to survey the market before purchasing. Find out who the top manufacturers are and become familiar with the most practical equipment features.

Basic Office Machines

The efficiency of any home office can be enhanced by the right choice of office machines. As a result of technological advancements, many of these machines now go beyond their original functions. Telephones and typewriters have become part of computer networks, answering machines can be accessed from outside your home, calculators can be programmed, and copiers now fit on desktops.

Because of the large number of features and options available with these standard office machines, you'll need to carefully assess your particular business needs to make the correct choices.

Telephones. In many businesses, as well as many households, the telephone is the most important and most frequently used piece of equipment. If your home business relies on clients, you well understand that the telephone can be a business lifeline.

The telephone has become so sophisticated in recent years that Alexander Graham Bell would probably no longer recognize his own invention. Some phones allow you to program frequently called numbers, so you can place a call by pressing a single button. Another option is "last number redial"—a real convenience when you reach a busy signal.

Other phones let you switch off the microphone in the handset so you can speak privately to someone in your office. And a speaker phone eliminates the need for a handset, leaving your hands free while you're talking on the phone (clarity and range vary with different models, so check them out carefully).

If the telephone is a key business machine for you, you may need two or three lines, especially if one will be taken over by a computer modem (see page 37). Your local telephone company can install extra lines for you. (If you decide to have two or more lines, you'll need a phone that can handle the extra traffic.)

Once the lines and jacks are in place, installing phones today simply means plugging them in. Keep in mind that there are some areas that do not operate on tone dialing. To ensure that your phone is completely adaptable, buy one with a pulse/tone switch.

Telephone answering machines. Nobody can stay near the telephone at all times, but you can do the next best thing by placing an answering machine in your office. With an answering machine, callers can hear the greeting you've recorded, then leave their own message on the machine's tape. To receive your messages, you simply play back the tape.

Answering machine options include an announce-only setting, which allows callers to hear a message but not leave one; call screening, which lets you know who's calling before you pick up the receiver; a digital display showing you the number of recorded messages; and voice-controlled operation (called VOX), which lets the caller talk as long as necessary, rather than within a time limit.

With a remote feature, you can receive messages while you're away from home. You just call your phone and activate the answering machine with a beeper, code word, or code number.

Typewriters. Like the telephone, the typewriter has undergone rapid change in this high-tech era. The original manual typewriter, with keys that you had to pound to make an imprint, has become obsolete as a practical piece of office equipment. Now, even its electric successor is quickly going the way of the manual, as the electronic typewriter takes over written communications.

With many computerlike operations, the electronic typewriter features a fast-moving daisy print wheel, the same mechanism used in letter-quality computer printers. The wheels are interchangeable, enabling you to use different typefaces. The electronic typewriter also has a

A Well-equipped Office

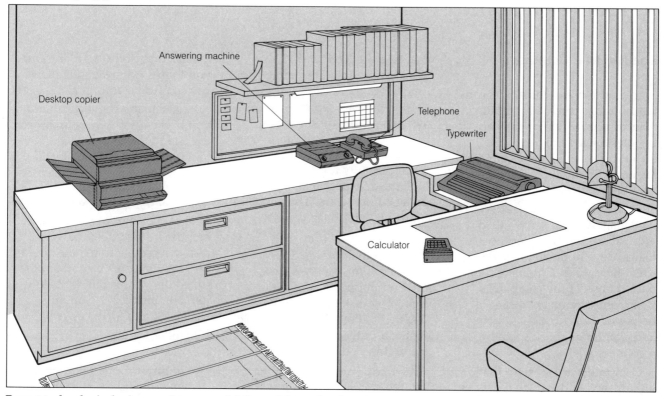

Desktop copier

Answering machine

Telephone

Typewriter

Calculator

Recent technological advances *have expanded the usefulness of such traditional office machines as the copier, telephone, typewriter, and calculator.*

memory; the amount of information that can be stored depends on the model.

With such a typewriter, correction is easy. Lines you've typed are viewed on a display panel and can be corrected before they're printed on paper. Some models even have a built-in spelling checker.

Deciding whether to buy an electronic typewriter, a computer, or both depends on your business needs and your budget. Keep in mind, though, that a typewriter can do just one job—word processing. A computer not only does word processing but a whole range of other jobs as well (see page 36).

Copiers. Until recently, copiers appeared only in large offices. Today, however, you can purchase small, desktop models that take up less than 1½ square feet of

space. Before you decide to purchase one, though, weigh its usefulness against the cost and convenience of your local copy shop.

Most copiers use ordinary paper and require toner and developer. Some models have removable cartridges (containing the toner, developer, and drum) that can be used for a specific number of copies before they must be replaced; you purchase new cartridges from an office supplier and replace them yourself.

A less expensive alternative is the dry copier, which uses no toner or developer. However, you have to purchase special coated paper, which increases the average cost per copy.

Features to consider when choosing a copier include easy maintenance, quick warm-up time, copy speed, the kind of paper required, the capacity

for both single-sheet and automatic paper feed, reduction/enlargement capability, and the ability to take different sizes of paper.

Calculators. Many desktop calculators include both a digital display and a paper printout. These calculators range from 3½ to 9½ inches wide, 7 to 12 inches deep, and 1½ to 3 inches high. Most operate on either AC current or rechargeable batteries.

Calculator options include 10- or 12-digit numeric display, a multiple-use key, a decimal setting selection, 3- or 4-key memory, and 2-color printout.

When you choose a calculator, try out the keys to make sure they're large enough and comfortably spaced for your hand. Also check the readability of the digital display.

...getting equipped

The Personal Computer

More and more home offices center around a personal computer. A most versatile office assistant, it handles a wide range of tasks, including word processing, record keeping, financial planning, and data interpretation.

Before you invest in a PC, you'll obviously want to know much more about the latest technological developments than we can cover here. Our simplified descriptions of the computer's basic components are meant to help you shop for a computer and plan home office space to accommodate it.

Computers are systems that link up several basic components, including the keyboard, disk drives, monitor, and printer. With some computers, each of these components is a separate unit. With others, the disk drive (or drives), keyboard, and monitor are housed in a single unit.

Plan carefully for the space you'll need, especially if you're buying components. They may require an extra-deep counter.

Disks and disk drives. Programmed information is stored either on floppy or hard disks. The floppy disk (also called a diskette or "floppy") is removable. Most computer software is available in floppy-disk form.

The hard disk is fixed rather than removable. It has a much greater capacity to store information than a floppy, and it allows you to retrieve information faster.

As the name suggests, the function of the disk drive is to drive the disk. One or two disk drives (often one for a hard disk and another for floppies) are usually built into a computer's CPU (central processing unit), which houses the computer's memory boards. It's helpful to have two disk drives: one to handle operating system software and another to handle your input data. With just one disk drive, you must shift back and forth between functions.

The monitor. Depending on the system you choose, the com-

A Computer Work Center

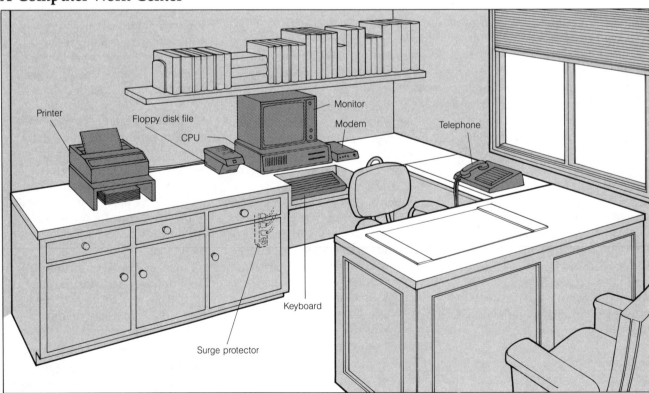

Setting up a computer *in your home office can present a challenge. Here, the office shown on the preceding page has been revamped to accommodate a computer and its typical peripheral equipment in a setup that assures user comfort.*

puter's viewing screen may be a separate unit or part of a larger unit that also houses the CPU and, in some systems, the keyboard. To give you an idea of dimensions, one popular separate monitor measures 14½ inches wide, 13½ inches deep, and 10 inches high.

The computer monitor resembles a television. And, like a television, it displays its information or graphics either in a monochrome or in color. (Some monitors can do both.) The monochrome shade may be amber, green, or white; all three are displayed on black backgrounds. The color monitor is, as a rule, more practical for graphic-design use than for display of text or figures.

When you choose a monitor, check the image carefully for clarity, keeping in mind that any focusing difficulty can result in eye strain.

The keyboard. The computer keyboard, through which information is inputted into the computer, generally has the same standard arrangement of letter and number keys as a typewriter. In addition, there are sometimes special function keys to command software and a numeral key pad identical to the one on a calculator. As with a typewriter or calculator, try out the keyboard before purchasing to make sure that it's comfortable under your hands and that the keys are large enough for your fingers.

In planning your office work surfaces, keep in mind that keyboards are generally 14 to 20 inches wide, 6 to 9 inches deep, and about 1½ inches high.

The printer. The two most common types of computer printers for home use are dot matrix and letter-quality.

The dot matrix printer forms images from controlled masses of pinpoint dots. It's smaller, faster,

quieter, and less expensive than most letter-quality printers, and it's particularly useful for graphics. But because the image produced by many dot matrix printers isn't sharp and precise, texts may not look as professional. However, double-strike dot matrix printers, which provide near-letter-quality printing, are also available. Dot matrix printers range from about 15 to 18 inches wide, 11½ to 13½ inches deep, and 3½ to 6½ inches high.

Letter-quality printers produce crisp, clear type. Variable typefaces revolve on a daisy print wheel or on a round element similar to the kind used in some typewriters. Many letter-quality printers are noisy, but special equipment can be purchased to quiet them. These printers tend to be slightly larger than dot matrix ones: 16½ to 25½ inches wide, 13 to 14 inches deep, and 4 to 6 inches high.

The modem. A revolutionary tool for many home businesses, the modem opens up computer access to the outside world. Through your telephone, you can transfer information from your home computer to another computer, any distance away. You can also contact on-line information services.

In choosing a modem, look for compatibility with your computer, your communications software, and the information services you might need to use.

Both internal modems that mount inside your computer and external modems are available. External types measure about 6 inches wide, 9 inches deep, and 2 inches high. The modem plugs into a regular telephone jack; the telephone plugs into the modem.

Protecting your computer. The computer's internal components are highly sensitive and can be

easily damaged by such everyday phenomena as static electricity and dust. But you can protect your computer with specialized products.

A jolt of static electricity can strike a computer's memory circuit like destructive lightning. A static protector can shield your computer from such damage. Grounded near the wall outlet, a static protector is a floor mat, table mat, or small touch plate attached to the computer. You simply touch it to release the static electricity before you touch the computer. Other antistatic options include antistatic carpeting or rubber matting placed under and around the computer.

Equally important for protecting your computer, a simple outlet box called a surge protector shields against the sudden surges of power that occasionally enter the house wiring or occur when a refrigerator or other large appliance suddenly switches off. Such jolts can damage a computer's memory. The surge protector plugs into your wall outlet, and the computer plugs into the protector.

Protection against power failure, on the other hand, is more a convenience to you. Though a power failure won't damage the computer, you will lose data if one occurs as you're feeding information into the computer, even if the failure is only momentary.

You can attach an uninterrupted power supply unit to your computer to provide a brief battery backup in case of power failure. With this device, you'll be able to save the work in progress on a disk.

Though electrical current, or the lack of it, can cause dramatic damage while you're working on a computer, don't underestimate the dangers of ordinary dust or animal hair. It's a good idea to protect the computer with a cover. Many attractive styles are available.

...getting equipped

Ergonomics at Work

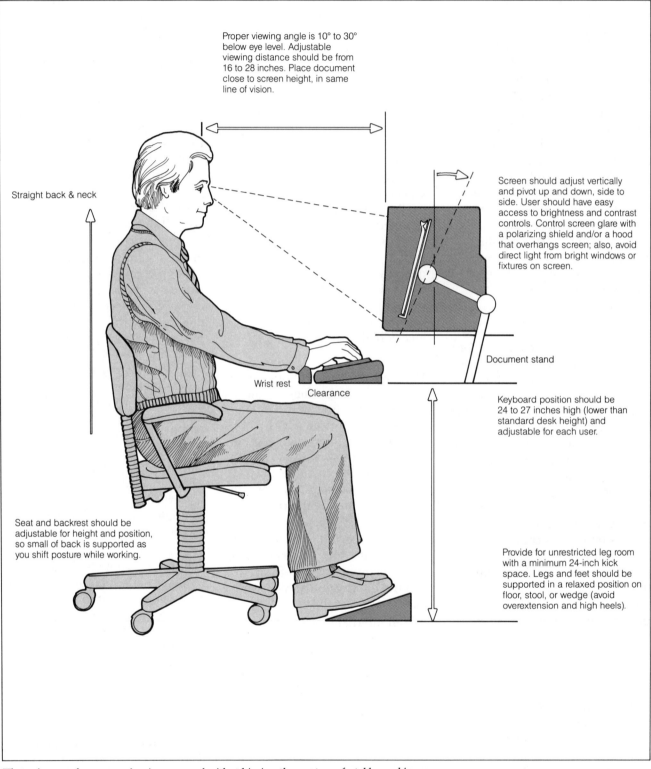

Proper viewing angle is 10° to 30° below eye level. Adjustable viewing distance should be from 16 to 28 inches. Place document close to screen height, in same line of vision.

Straight back & neck

Screen should adjust vertically and pivot up and down, side to side. User should have easy access to brightness and contrast controls. Control screen glare with a polarizing shield and/or a hood that overhangs screen; also, avoid direct light from bright windows or fixtures on screen.

Wrist rest

Clearance

Document stand

Keyboard position should be 24 to 27 inches high (lower than standard desk height) and adjustable for each user.

Seat and backrest should be adjustable for height and position, so small of back is supported as you shift posture while working.

Provide for unrestricted leg room with a minimum 24-inch kick space. Legs and feet should be supported in a relaxed position on floor, stool, or wedge (avoid overextension and high heels).

The science of ergonomics *is concerned with achieving the most comfortable working relationship possible between people and the machines they use. The guidelines above have been shown to ease strain during hours of intense concentration at a computer terminal.*

Office Furniture

In the past, standard office furniture tended to be heavy and unattractive, in "businesslike" colors ranging from buff and brown to gray and black. Today's office furniture, however, is both lighter and brighter, with new elegance, a wide array of color choices, and impressive design variety. Its sophistication shows up not only in appearance but also in function and comfort.

Read through this section to learn about basic office furnishings. Then turn to the "Office Showcase," beginning on page 43, for a look at some of the top office furniture designs currently available.

Selecting pieces. In choosing home office furnishings, a number of factors need to be considered. In the case of a desk, for example, size is often of primary importance. But you'll also want to investigate the desk's storage capacity, work surface, and such optional features as pull-out shelves. Quality, durability, and appearance also warrant investigation.

Because home office furniture gets hard, intensive use, it's important to scrutinize each piece carefully before purchase.

Ergonomics. The term *ergonomics* refers to human engineering— that is, designing equipment, furniture, and workspaces to be both efficient and comfortable for human use.

Until recently, little attention was paid to such concerns. But as computer use accelerated, workers spending long hours at terminals began to show signs of physical strain that had never before been associated with desk work. Complaints of backaches, headaches, neck and shoulder tension, eye strain, and general irritability led to the emergence of the ergonomics design field. Its aim was to study the characteristics of people in a working environment so safe, efficient work areas and equipment could be designed for them.

The findings of ergonomists, some of which are discussed below and illustrated on the facing page, are a helpful guide to choosing comfortable home office furniture.

Ergonomists have determined that for writing and other general paper work, the work surface should be 28½ inches from the floor. However, for comfortable typing or working at a computer keyboard, the work surface should stand 24 to 27 inches from the floor. This height enables you to type with both arms relaxed at your sides.

To protect against eye strain, a computer monitor should be located 16 to 28 inches from the operator's face. A turntable that allows the monitor to swivel or adjust to different angles is helpful. The copy holder should be the same distance away as the monitor to avoid eye strain from shifts of focus.

Choosing a desk chair is especially important, since you're likely to spend a lot of time sitting. It's best to try out various models in stores to see which are the most comfortable, but there are several ergonomic factors you'll want to consider, too. A chair with adjustable height will allow you to type comfortably, as well as work comfortably at your desk. Lumbar support is also important, so make sure that your chair firmly supports the small of the back. A cushioned chair should have firm rather than soft upholstery.

If you often work at a computer for hours at a stretch, use a foot stool and wrist rests to help relieve tension.

Storage Options

In a home office, the need for adequate storage is particularly acute. Without it, important documents, correspondence, and supplies can easily get mislaid or damaged.

Today's office designers offer a range of storage accommodations for everything from sharpened pencils to art boards. All you need to do is determine your needs and the available space.

Planning ahead. As you try to anticipate the amount of storage you'll need, think in generous terms. It's much more common to get into the bind of having too little storage than to have too much.

Make lists of what you need to store, right down to paper clips. Every kind of work has its own storage inventory, whether it's piles of periodicals for a writer or fabric and wallpaper samples for an interior designer.

In addition to this specialized storage, virtually every business requires file drawers to organize and protect correspondence and other important papers. And remember to include storage space for office supplies.

Storage styles. The same style spectrum evidenced in office furniture is available in storage units. At one end of the spectrum, office suppliers offer an ornate cabinet, called a "credenza," intended to supplement a simple desk or work table. At the simpler end of the spectrum are every useful size and shape of unadorned steel cabinets.

If you prefer to create your own storage style, you can use anything that works—from a steamer trunk for files to an umbrella stand for rolls of blueprints. One benefit of working at home is that you often enjoy a freer choice of office style.

Finding Office Space

Many people today live in homes of modest size and simple design. What space we have is quickly filled up with the clutter of domestic life. Finding even a few square feet for a home office can present a difficult challenge.

In the following section, you'll discover several different approaches to meeting this challenge. Let these ideas help you examine your home from top to bottom, both indoors and out, to find potential office space that you may have overlooked.

Factors to Consider

Before you rush off to empty the linen closet or measure the basement, work out on paper a rough plan for the kind of office space you're looking for. Start by writing out a list of what you consider to be the essential features of your future office space. Obviously, the kind of work you intend to do in your office will determine many of these features. Some will fall into the category of structural requirements; others will be related more to your comfort and personal work habits. All are equally critical to a successful office.

Discussed below are several examples of factors you'll want to consider in planning your home office.

Space. This is a top priority in selecting an office location, especially if your work takes up a lot of room or if you plan to share an office. Though you can write a thriller or make sales calls from the cozy confines of a renovated closet, seating half a dozen clients at a conference table calls for a considerably larger space. If you know that your work will require certain pieces of furniture or other equipment, be sure to keep their dimensions in mind as you evaluate possible office locations.

Electrical power. Your proposed office space must, of course, have adequate electrical power for your equipment and lighting demands. To determine your electrical needs, you'll need to know the major pieces of equipment you plan to use.

The most significant consumer of electricity will be the computer; if you'll be using one in your office, be sure that the office area's existing wiring is sufficient to handle the extra load. Some experts recommend that a computer have its own circuit.

Heating, cooling, and ventilation. These are obviously important both for physical comfort and for good health. To work at your highest level of efficiency, regardless of the task, the air temperature and humidity should be moderate.

Beware of locating your office in an uninsulated and inadequately cooled attic; in hot weather, such a space can become a furnace. Basements and garages, too, often need upgrading; they're frequently damp and inadequately heated.

If you use a computer and live in an area where temperatures are very high, air conditioning may be necessary no matter where your office is located—not only for your comfort but also for the protection of delicate floppy disks.

Windows. One or more windows can be a necessity for many home office workers. People who work for long hours at a computer, for example, need visual breaks in order to avoid eye strain and headaches. Also, many who work at home full-time find they need to combat a sense of isolation, especially if contact with other people is limited during the work week. For artists and designers, the natural light afforded by windows may be essential.

A separate entrance. If you'll be receiving clients, you may want a separate entrance for your home office. This can help keep your business activities from interfering with your domestic life, create a more businesslike impression with visitors, and protect your family's privacy.

Quiet. A valued working condition for many people, quiet is a two-way consideration for a home office, where keeping work noise confined to the office may be as important as keeping unwanted noise out.

Just how quiet your work area needs to be depends on the nature of your tasks and your powers of concentration. Some people bustle through a productive day listening to music, while others require complete silence.

You'll also want to consider the needs of your family. Even if your office is located a distance from the bedrooms, the racket of a computer printer spewing out

Where in the House?

Upstairs, downstairs, *and in every room along the way, you can find potential office space to adopt, adapt, borrow, or steal. Just start looking.*

...finding office space

data late at night could well disturb family members.

If you're concerned that noise will be a problem, plan on soundproofing the walls of the office. A soundproofing box is also available for computer printers.

The Search Is On

Most of us are so familiar with our homes that we tend to overlook potential office space staring us right in the face. Discovering usable space requires searching with a fresh point of view.

Whether squeezed from an existing room or annexed from thin air, office space exists in almost every home. Here are a few suggestions of areas that, with vision and diligence, can be converted into a home office. You'll also find a wealth of ideas in the photographs in the first chapter, "Finding a Space to Work," pages 4–31.

Spare rooms. The most obvious—and often the most advantageous—office space may be a rarely used guest room or den. If you're lucky enough to have a spare room, it probably lies outside the family's main traffic pattern, and it will usually require no structural improvements—just new furnishings. Another advantage is that a complete room is generally large enough to handle whatever furniture and equipment your office requires.

Shared spaces. One of the simplest home office setups, though it requires more careful planning than using a spare room, is taking over a portion of an existing room. For example, you might appropriate one wall of a bedroom, one end of an L-shaped

family room, the dining room's bay window, the far end of a hall, or the kitchen's breakfast area. Modular office units are available that can create an office space within a larger area.

Hand-me-down space. As children grow up and move out of the nest, many homes acquire vacant space in the form of outgrown bedrooms and playrooms; even family rooms can sometimes be recycled.

Closets. In many homes, there's often at least one large closet that can be liberated from its everyday occupation. Such closets offer gold mines of space when they're opened up and creatively reorganized. With the addition of some carefully designed built-ins, even a small, shallow closet can be turned into a compact home office.

Other interior spaces. A few more potential office spaces that tend to be overlooked include lofts and galleries, stairway landings, the space under a staircase, and basement and attic areas (though these must often be upgraded).

Exterior possibilities. Sometimes the most likely office space awaits your discovery outdoors rather than indoors. An exterior location provides the obvious advantage of greater separation from your domestic life, which may also result in more quiet and fewer interruptions.

To take advantage of exterior space, consider taking over all or part of the garage (or adding to it) or walling in a framed porch. Perhaps a little-used guest house could become the place to hang your shingle.

Evaluating Your New Space

Once you've found an apparently suitable space for your office, compare its features with your list of requirements. Check the space for structural soundness. If it will need remodeling, read "Working with Professionals" on pages 62–63 to get an idea of what is involved.

To ensure that the proposed office space will meet your needs, subject it to the following questions:

- Are the area's heating, cooling, and ventilation systems adequate to handle your office requirements?

- Will you need to upgrade the electrical circuitry or add a telephone line?

- Is the lighting—both natural and artificial—sufficient? Are there problems with glare?

- If you expect clients to call on you, does the space project a suitable image or will remodeling or redecorating be necessary?

- Does the space now, or will it after remodeling, meet local building codes? (Check with your local building inspector before making any structural changes.)

- Does the space please you? Will you be able to work in it comfortably and efficiently?

If, after reasonable compromises, you find that your proposed office location passes inspection, you're ready to turn your dreams into hard-working reality. The following sections of this chapter will give you invaluable guidelines, and the color photographs on pages 4–31 and 64–79 will provide ideas and inspiration.

Office Furniture Showcase

From traditional to trendy, there are so many styles and features available in office furnishings today that the choice range can satisfy every taste and need.

Making the right decisions about furnishings for your office is crucial. Each choice you make has the potential to influence your efficiency and morale; both, in turn, can affect your business success. Since a large chunk of each work day, for many of us, is spent in the comfort—or at the mercy—of office furniture, pieces that serve us well are a wise investment.

This eight-page section presents an illustrated guide to the basic categories of office furniture most in demand today. Let them help you as you decide upon the most practical choices for your situation. Look for these furnishings at office supply outlets, large stationery stores, and furniture showrooms.

Modular Wall Systems

From its origin in northern Europe, the modular wall system has spread throughout the Western world, answering today's demand for well-designed nomadic furnishings. Based on modular units that work like building blocks, a system can be designed in a number of different configurations. The idea is to tailor the system to fit individual needs and the available space.

A great problem solver, the modular wall system produces quality home offices virtually out of thin air. It can smoothly meet the special demands of an office that shares space with a bedroom or other living area, or it can squeeze maximum use from a small room. And if, like many people today, you eventually uproot and move to a new location, the system can easily travel with you.

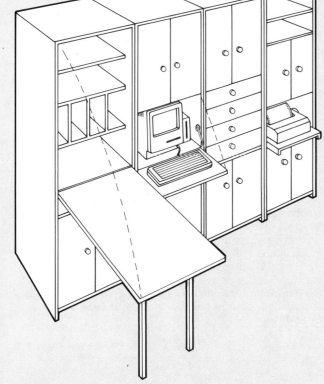

Available with or without a variety of extras, modular wall systems are usually designed to be closed up at the end of the working day. As shown in the illustration at left, desks swing down when needed, then up and out of sight when your paperwork is done. Files and equipment slide out for service, then in for storage.

The main advantage of a modular wall system is its versatility. Besides accommodating every peripheral for your computer, from mouse to modem, such a system can even cache a Murphy bed (see page 7). Some dealers will custom-design a system to suit your type of work and available wall space. You may also want to extend the system's functions to house home entertainment equipment or a family library.

Desks

Because a desk is generally the bulkiest piece of office furniture, it's usually the first to be positioned in an office. Its size and design not only affect the way you work but can also have a psychological impact on others. A big, executive desk evokes authority, for example, while an open, table-style desk may invite freer discussion.

Standard desk height is 29 inches, the measurement found to be comfortable for most people when they perform general office tasks. Antique desks and writing tables may stand slightly higher or lower. If you're taller or shorter than average, be sure to sit down and try out any desk before purchasing it. If a desk seems too high or too low, remember that an adjustable chair can make it more comfortable (see page 46).

Most people type more comfortably at slightly lower work surfaces; the recommended height for both type-writers and computer keyboards is 24 to 27 inches above the floor. Office desks sometimes accommodate a type-writer on a right- or left-hand return, a shelf or projection that sits at a right angle to the desk.

Desk dimensions other than height vary greatly, from large and imposing to trim and dainty. Some desks are manufactured specifically for office use; others are for more casual work in a home study, family room, or bedroom. Specialty furniture outlets, such as those featuring Scandinavian or Italian designs, offer a variety of beautiful desks. Also check office supply outlets and large stationery stores.

Style	Characteristics
Standard Office Styles 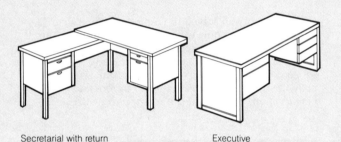 Secretarial with return Executive	Secretarial desks come in a wide variety of styles. The type shown in the illustration, with a return for a typewriter, is especially popular. Often made with a natural or simulated hardwood finish, executive desks are categorized mainly by size. Large desktops can measure 72 by 36 inches; a more typical size would be 60 by 30 inches. Conference-style desks are designed so that the top overhangs by several inches the area where a client would sit.
Traditional Styles 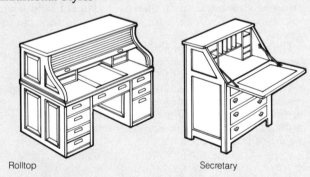 Rolltop Secretary	Shown here are two desks derived from the fashions of the eighteenth and nineteenth centuries, when business communications were handwritten with pen and ink. These desks serve principally as writing tables, though they offer storage space, as well. These traditional desks lend warmth and elegance to home offices. Both the rolltop and the secretary allow you to shut projects-in-progress out of sight, and both are lockable.
Contemporary Designs 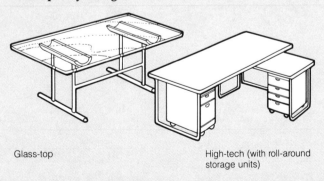 Glass-top High-tech (with roll-around storage units)	What sets contemporary office designs apart are their responsiveness to today's ways of doing business and their freedom from convention. Many contemporary desks, such as the glass-top model shown in the illustration, are much lighter and more open in feeling than the designs of the past. Gleaming chrome, slick laminates, and surprising colors and styling have all brought desk design into the forefront of fashion. If a sharp, contemporary image is important to your business or suits your taste, choose from this group.

Computer Work Centers

Anyone who has spent several hours at a computer that's been set up on a standard office desk can appreciate the benefits of specially designed computer furniture.

Regardless of the amount of time you spend working at your computer, you may find that your existing desk can't comfortably handle all the necessary equipment. You may also want the freedom of being able to roll the computer into other rooms so other members of the family can use it. In both cases, a specially designed computer work center can be the perfect solution.

How does a work center differ from a regular desk? Since a computer involves a cluster of equipment, work centers are designed on several levels (either fixed or movable), and work surfaces are placed at heights that are ergonomically correct for the job at hand. (The illustration on page 38 explains the ergonomic principles involved in working at a computer keyboard.)

Before you purchase a work center, you should already have purchased or chosen your computer, since the work center needs to fit your computer and its peripheral equipment. The work center must also fit you, so sit down and try it out to be sure it's comfortable.

Valuable work center options include built-in wrist rests and surfaces with adjustable heights and angles, such as a tilting turntable for the monitor. Make sure that there are enough openings for electrical cables and large enough slots for paper in the area where the printer will sit. Many work centers even come equipped with shelves where you can store computer manuals and documentation or extra computer supplies.

Most computer furniture is constructed of wood, often with a veneer of oak, teak, or walnut. You can purchase attractive, ready-made pieces at computer stores or other retail outlets or have a design custom-built for you.

Style	Characteristics
Mobile	The computer has come into its own so quickly that many new users don't quite know what to do with it in their homes. Setting the computer up in its own portable work center gives it the flexibility required when it's being used by several members of the family.

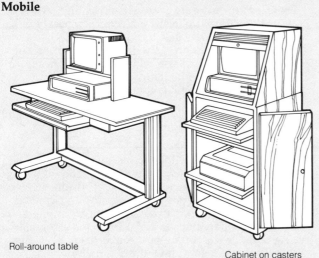

Roll-around table

Cabinet on casters

The roll-around table features a slide-out shelf to accommodate the keyboard at the appropriate height. The monitor sits on what's called a bridge. The cabinet on casters is a good design for people with limited space. Both the keyboard and the printer slide out for use and in for storage. At the end of the day, the pull-down lid and cabinet doors lock all the equipment safely away.

Stationary

When the computer is integral to your home office, you'll probably opt to keep it in one place, using a stationary work center such as one of those illustrated at left. The emphasis here is on your working comfort and efficiency.

The larger, L-shaped corner unit offers generous working space. The triangular corner piece allows you to use space that would otherwise be wasted. The shorter leg of the L holds the printer.

The smaller, compact unit is a standard computer desk commonly sold at computer furniture outlets. A computer on such a unit can be placed in almost any room without intrusion.

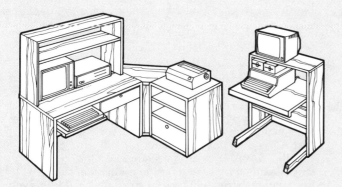

Corner unit

Compact unit

Desk Chairs

Office planners have estimated that people spend as much as 75 percent of a typical work day seated in a chair. Obviously, if suitable seating is not provided, the body will suffer stress and strain.

A well-designed chair demonstrates the principles of ergonomics better than any other piece of office furniture. Good-quality desk chairs are adjustable and mobile while providing firm support. Look for a chair that moves with you as you shift in it, supporting you both as you lean forward to type or write and when you sink back to talk on the phone.

Good ergonomic designs have a firm springiness in the base and backrest to keep you from jarring your spine. The seat cushion should be slightly rounded in front, rather firm, and covered in a porous fabric (rather than vinyl). Also, be sure that the chair's seat height is adjustable.

Most people prefer casters on a desk chair for mobility. Make sure that your chair rolls smoothly on the flooring under your desk. Keep in mind that a five-legged chair base is more stable than one with four legs.

An alternative to traditional desk chairs, the BALANS chair was specially designed to relieve back pressure and ensure proper posture. Two versions are shown below.

Style	Characteristics
Armchairs	Office armchairs, also known as executive chairs, tend to be big, roomy, and comfortable. Before you purchase one of these chairs, make sure that your desk can accommodate it and that your office layout allows adequate clearance.

Standard armchairs are characterized by high, wide backs and luxurious upholstery. Most swing back, like a rocker, and swivel from side to side or in a full circle.

The ergonomic version of the armchair features a properly contoured backrest, adjustability, and firmly cushioned support, without sacrificing comfort or luxury. Both standard and ergonomic armchairs come with casters.

Standard   Ergonomic

Typing Chairs

Typing chairs are built without arms, because arms interfere with a typist's movements. The standard typing chair comes in wood, metal, or plastic. Its distinction is obvious—it's simple, lightweight, and mobile. Standard typing chairs usually don't give the best back support.

For more comfort and support, turn to the ergonomic typing chair. Its supporting post contains a gas cylinder that both adjusts height and buffers impact.

Standard   Ergonomic

BALANS Chairs

Adjustable   Rocking

The BALANS chair, a recent innovation from Norway, was developed by designer Petter Opsvik in conjunction with medical specialists in back care. Their objective was to provide a chair that eases pressure on the back and at the same time promotes proper posture. Their successful design has been much imitated.

With a BALANS chair, you sit on a seat that tilts your torso slightly forward and rest your knees on cushions. Even without structural back support, the chair keeps your back straight and free of strain.

Drafting Tables & Stools

The specialized tables and stools shown below are just as important to the architects, designers, and draftspeople who use them as the office desk is to a bookkeeper, lawyer, or writer. People who work at drafting tables require freedom of arm and torso movement over the entire surface of the table. They need a table that's sturdy and a work surface that's durable, flat, and smooth. They also want to be able to adjust the surface infinitesimally— up and down, at different angles, and even side to side.

For these and other reasons, the drafting table and its stool could be considered tools of the design trades rather than furniture. Many types are available, several of which are displayed below. Shop carefully to be sure your table and stool will meet your particular work requirements.

Style	Characteristics
Professional Tables 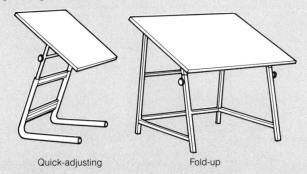 Hydraulic Counter-balanced	You can automatically adjust the quality drafting tables shown at left by operating one or more pedals at the base. The hydraulic type allows you to shift height, angle, and side-to-side position effortlessly. The counterbalanced table, also pedal-controlled, includes a foot rail for people who work standing up. These and other heavy, professional-quality drafting tables have interchangeable tops of varying size made of wood or plastic-laminated fiberboard. Artists sometimes protect the work surface with inexpensive and disposable sheets of vinyl.
Lightweight Tables  Quick-adjusting Fold-up	The tables shown at left are much less expensive and lighter in weight than the professional tables discussed above. Not intended to last a lifetime, these tables must be manually adjusted, but they have the advantage of folding up for easy storage. Like their professional counterparts, lightweight tables generally adjust in both height and tilt, and offer a range of interchangeable tops.
Drafting Stools Adjustable Standard	To work at a drafting table, people sit, stand, or do some combination of the two. For this reason, a high drafting stool, rather than a standard desk chair, is usually preferred. A good drafting stool should support a person's free and easy movement across the work surface. Some people prefer an adjustable stool; by operating a lever under the seat, you can move the chair up or down. Whether you use a standard stool design or a special model, a footrest is helpful, since your feet may not reach the floor. As with a desk chair, having arms may prove more comfortable, but be sure they don't interfere with your working motions.

Storage Units

The paper and other materials generated by most office work can quickly become overwhelming if you don't have adequate storage. For most offices, the primary storage concerns are where to file papers and where to store office supplies. (Storage of books is discussed on the facing page.)

It's most convenient to store papers such as correspondence, bills, and other written matter in file cabinets. With a carefully organized filing system, these papers will not only be securely stored but also readily accessible when needed.

When it comes to storing office supplies—stationery, pens and pencils, packages of paper, typewriter or printer ribbons—you can be much more creative. Options run the gamut from plastic milk crates to carved wood armoires.

Whatever you need to store, be sure to choose containers that adequately protect the material and allow easy access to it.

Style	Characteristics

File Cabinets

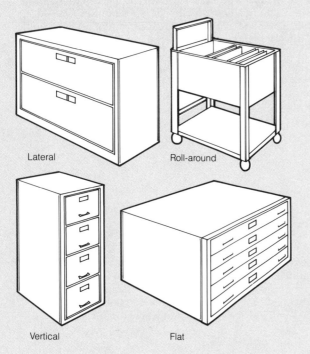

Lateral

Roll-around

Vertical

Flat

Standard office file cabinets, designed to hold either regular- or legal-size papers, come with drawers arranged either vertically or laterally. Vertical files are both more traditional and more commonly used. Their depths range from 14 to 25 inches; their height depends on the number of drawers in the cabinet.

Lateral file cabinets have an average depth of 19 inches and vary in width from 30 to 42 inches. Because of their greater width, they command more wall space than vertical file cabinets. Stacked in tiers of two or three drawers, lateral file cabinets can double as a room divider. Make sure that only one drawer at a time can be opened to protect against tipping.

A roll-around file cabinet can usually hide under a desk or counter when not needed. Some models include a hinged top and a lower file drawer.

Flat files, with their deep, wide drawers, are designed to protect the paper and art boards used by architects, designers, and others. It's important that the drawers glide smoothly and easily, preferably on ball bearings.

Supply Storage

Metal cabinet

Converted armoire

Suitable storage for office supplies depends on the nature of your business, the size of your home office, and the amount of supplies you need to store. Beyond this, the choice of containers depends solely on your personal taste and whim. Almost anything will work as supply storage, as long as it protects your materials and keeps them easily accessible.

Some home offices, such as those occupying an outgrown child's room, come equipped with built-in supply storage in the form of roomy closets. Sometimes a cabinet can be built into a wall. You can also purchase many types and styles of storage furniture from contemporary designs to antique cabinets. Two examples are shown here.

Shelving

Whether stacked to the ceiling in a dozen horizontal layers or aligned as an inconspicuous pair, shelves are a useful addition to almost every office. Though most often filled with books, manuals, periodicals, and the like, shelves also make handy repositories for office supplies, plants, and even knickknacks.

Beyond their functional purpose, shelves can give a warm, finished appearance to an office. Used in moderation, they enrich a small, otherwise undistinguished space. Too many shelves, on the other hand, especially in a room lacking a window, can turn coziness into claustrophobia. Most important of all, shelves are very versatile—when there isn't enough floor space, they can be mounted on a wall. And you can have them in a myriad of different heights and widths.

Starting with the basic styles shown in the illustrations below, you can find a variety of practical shelves to fit every situation. You can even have shelves custom-designed to fit under windows, over doors, inside closets, and into oddly shaped spaces.

Style

Wall-mounted

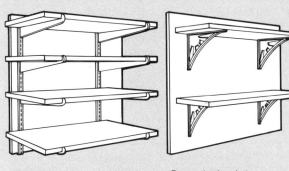

Tracks & brackets   Decorative brackets

Characteristics

Inexpensive and easy to install, wall-mounted shelving has two other advantages: it's flexible, allowing you to place any number of shelves wherever needed, and it has a lighter appearance than most other shelving styles.

The track and bracket style allows you to tailor a complex shelving system to fit your specific needs. The tracks need to be bolted into wall studs to support the weight of the shelves and the items stored on them.

Large, decorative brackets are more attractive, but they're less flexible. Here, you bolt the brackets themselves to the studs.

Freestanding

Industrial shelving   Bookcase

Shown at left are only two of the many types of freestanding shelves available. These substantial pieces of furniture can also serve secondary roles as room dividers or as extra counter space.

Industrial shelving typically is made of metal. Bookcases are available in unfinished wood, wood veneer, brightly enameled metal, and other high-tech dressings.

Built-in

Tracks & clips

Built-in shelving has a clean, smoothly integrated appearance that often intrudes less upon an office layout and decorative style than other shelving options. Commonly placed in the hollow space between wall studs, built-in shelves also allow you to make full use of office space that might otherwise go to waste.

Mounting the shelves on tracks and clips lets you arrange the shelves in exactly the configuration you need.

Desk Lamps

Lighting comes from two different sources: from the sun streaming through windows (natural light) and from the bulb of an electrical fixture (artificial light). The focus here is on artificial light, and more specifically on task lighting (explained on pages 57–58).

The concentrated task lighting from a desk lamp can have a powerful impact on your office. Because it affects your visual comfort, your general efficiency, and the overall look of your surroundings, you'll want to choose your desk lamp with special care.

Style

Characteristics

Incandescent

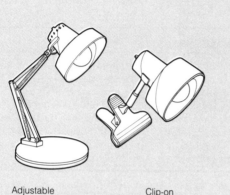

Adjustable   Clip-on

Incandescent light, the most common type used in homes, is produced by a tungsten thread that burns slowly inside the familiar glass bulb. The glow produced is generally considered to be more flattering to people's skin coloring than the light from a fluorescent bulb. However, incandescent bulbs use more energy and produce more heat than their fluorescent counterparts.

The shape of the lamp shades at left indicates that the fixtures were designed to hold pear-shaped incandescent bulbs. Both lamps have adjustable necks that allow you to direct task lighting where it's needed.

Fluorescent

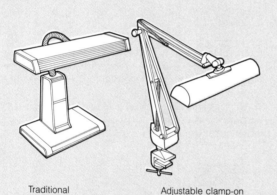

Traditional   Adjustable clamp-on

Fluorescent light is produced when electrical energy and mercury vapor create an arc that stimulates the phosphors coating the bulb interior. Long favored for office use, fluorescent light is cooler than incandescent light, as well as three times as energy-efficient. Fluorescent tubes last 5 to 20 times as long as their incandescent equivalents.

Both desk lamps shown at left use the typical long fluorescent tube. The traditional model stands in a stationary position, usually at the center back of the desk. The adjustable type can be shifted in every direction, from the shade and neck down to the swiveling base, and can be clamped conveniently to a desk or table.

Specialized

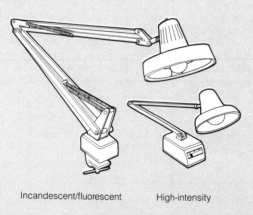

Incandescent/fluorescent   High-intensity

For close-up work and other specialized task-lighting needs, there are numerous desk lamp designs available. The large, fully adjustable clamp-on lamp with two bulbs is preferred by people who need a full, balanced wash of light. The incandescent bulb at the center, which casts a pinkish glow, is encircled by a round fluorescent bulb that has a bluish cast.

The smaller lamp, a high-intensity type, is valued by people who are short on space but long on lighting needs. Its tiny bulb sends a concentrated beacon of light where it's needed with a simple adjustment of the lamp's base, neck, or shade.

Designing Your Office

When all the individual aspects of home office planning are brought together in a workable and pleasing arrangement, a final design scheme emerges. A good home office plan will accommodate the way you want to work and the kinds of furniture and equipment you'll be using in the space you have available.

There are few universal rules to guide your office design—you must start with your own unique situation. The space you've chosen for your home office may require only a fresh coat of paint, or it may need an architect's expertise. Whatever the case, you can use this section to plot your way to a practical plan.

Drawing Plans

The first step in designing your office is drawing plans, both from a bird's-eye view and from a straight-on perspective. Whether you rely on a professional or do all the designing and building yourself, these detailed plans will save you time and money, and will help you work out the best possible office arrangement.

Taking accurate measurements. The accuracy of your plans directly affects the success of your finished home office design, and accurate drawing requires the proper tools. You can purchase the following items at hardware, stationery, or art supply stores.

- Retractable steel measuring tape or carpenter's rule
- Ruler or T-square
- Triangle
- Compass or circle template
- Graph paper (squares no smaller than 4 per inch)
- Masking tape
- Pencils
- Eraser
- Clipboard or pad with 8½- by 11-inch paper

Since a difference in space of even a few inches can cramp the swivel of your desk chair, accuracy both in measuring and in recording the measurements is crucial to developing a useful plan. Be sure to double-check each measurement.

Making rough sketches. Before you can design an efficient and complete workspace, you'll need a floor plan (a bird's-eye view) of the room and one or more elevation drawings (straight-on views of each wall). To draw these plans accurately, you first must make a rough sketch of the floor plan and of any elevations.

To begin your sketch of the floor plan, make a rough outline of the perimeter of the office area. Using most of the paper, show any doors, windows, recesses, and projections that are in the space. Then, as you take each measurement, write it down on this rough sketch; later, you'll transfer the dimensions to your finished plans.

Start your measurements at one corner of a wall, measuring from the corner to the first window frame's outer edge. From this point, measure to the opposite edge of the window frame and then from the opposite edge of the frame to the far corner.

Make any intermediate measurements needed to indicate a heating vent, closet, or any other feature of the wall. Note the locations of all electrical outlets, switches, and telephone jacks.

All of these measurements can be transferred directly onto your rough sketch of each elevation. In addition, you'll need to measure and record window and door heights, as well as the height of the ceiling. Be sure to note any ceiling slope or other unusual wall configuration.

Repeat the process for each wall in turn, making sure you have all the dimensions you'll need.

Drawing a floor plan. A floor plan provides a background against which you can visualize, measure, and plot the best office layout.

To draw the floor plan from your rough sketch, you'll need graph paper; its squares will represent units of measurement. Most architects use graph paper with a scale of ¼ inch to 1 foot. However, you may find it easier to use graph paper with larger, ½-inch squares (allowing ½ inch to the foot); also, a larger drawing gives you more room for writing down dimensions and labels.

With masking tape, attach the graph paper at each corner to a smooth drawing board or work surface. Follow the rough sketch you've made. If one wall, for example, measured 12 feet, 3 inches long, you would mark off 12¼ squares of graph paper for the length of that wall.

Use a ruler or T-square to draw horizontal lines. For vertical lines at a perfect right angle (such as a

...designing your office

Sample Floor Plan & Elevation

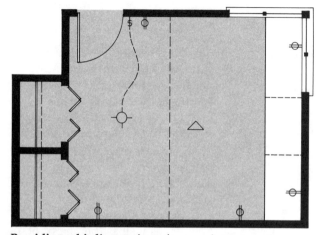

Providing a bird's-eye view *of a space drawn to scale, a floor plan delineates every wall, aperture, outlet, and switch—in short, almost every structural detail.*

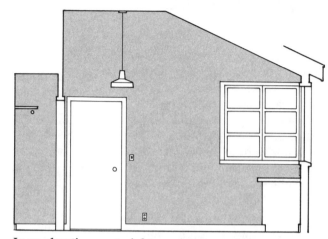

In an elevation or straight-on view, *every feature on a wall, including doors and windows, outlets, switches, and the ceiling line, is carefully drawn to scale.*

corner of the room), use a triangle with one edge placed over the horizontal line. To account for the space taken up by a door, set a compass to the scaled-down door's width and use it to draw the door's direction of swing.

Designate additional features using the architectural symbols shown below. Examine the sample floor plan above to see what a completed scale drawing looks like.

Drawing elevations. A head-on view, an elevation shows how a room looks to a person standing in the middle of the floor, facing one wall. The purpose of an elevation is to allow you to plan the best arrangement of cabinets, equipment, and other additions against each wall in relation to such features as windows, doors, electrical outlets, and vents.

Using your rough elevation sketch (or sketches) with all

dimensions measured, double-checked, and recorded, you're ready to transfer the measurements to graph paper, just as you did for the floor plan. Make sure you use the same scale for the elevations as you did for the floor plan.

Start by drawing the perimeter of each wall. Next, fill in all the fixed features, such as windows, light fixtures, telephone jacks, and electrical outlets.

Architectural Symbols

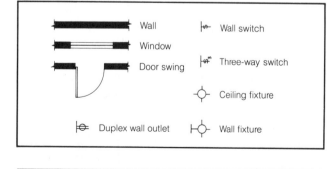

Architects and designers use a set of standard symbols to indicate certain features on floor plans; some of the most common ones are shown at left. You'll find them useful for adding essential information to your floor plan without cluttering it with written labels.

Elements of Good Design

Your floor plan and elevations are but a skeletal design for your future home office. To arrive at a final design that will work comfortably for you in the years ahead requires detailed planning.

The four functions basic to most office work are telephoning, desk work, computer keyboard operation and/or typing, and storage. Of course, your own work may involve different or additional tasks. Make a list of the tasks specific to your occupation and visualize or act out each activity to determine its special space requirements.

Adapted to your specific situation, the following general guidelines can help you design an efficient and comfortable home office.

Positioning furniture. Decide which direction you want to face as you sit at your desk or work surface. If you crave privacy, you may prefer to have your back to the door. Or it may be important to you to locate your desk so you can look out a window.

Plan for work surfaces that are at least 22 inches deep. If you type or use a word processor regularly, you'll need at least 18 inches of clear space on one or both sides of the machine for copy.

Be sure to plan enough clearance between furnishings so you can maneuver easily. Also check to see that at least 32 inches of walking space is available between seating for visitors and the door. And plan for the clearance required by the entrance door as well as cabinet drawers and doors.

Locating basic equipment. Plan the location of each major piece of equipment you'll be using. Turn to pages 38 and 39 to review the ergonomic recommendations for a computer (or typewriter) keyboard and monitor.

In planning for a printer or copier, make allowances for both its bulk and its appetite for paper (and the way the paper feeds).

The telephone is a home office lifeline, and its position should be planned carefully. Some experts recommend that, if you're right-handed, you place the phone near your left side as you sit at your desk. Then, if you jot on a pad as you talk on the phone, its cord won't pull across your body and your right hand will be free. If you're left-handed, reverse the position.

Plan for safe and unobtrusive electrical and telephone hookups. You might want to conceal computer cables and electrical cords with furniture, but be sure all switches and outlets are easily accessible.

Laying Out Your Office

With your floor plan and elevations complete and the elements of design duly considered, you're ready to make a layout of your home office. As already discussed, the "right layout" is a flexible concept that changes according to the variables of each individual situation. Personal preferences and work habits are key factors, as are the size and location of the office space and the kind of work to be done there.

For ideas on some basic layouts, study the sample floor plans on pages 54–55.

Making scale cutouts. Easy and fun to make, scale cutouts allow you to experiment with every conceivable layout before deciding on the one which will work best for you.

To make scale cutouts, first measure each piece of furniture and equipment necessary to your future office, following the same procedure used to draw up the floor plan and elevations. Using graph paper of the same scale as your plans, draw scale models of each piece. Samples of such models are shown on page 56.

Coloring each scale model so it will stand out against the floor plan is helpful. Also, make sure you label each piece.

Arranging the pieces. Using your floor plan as a background, place the cutouts where you think each piece of furniture or equipment will prove most convenient.

As you study the possibilities, you'll probably see places where compromise will result in just the right layout. In fact, you may arrive at more than one suitable arrangement. Make duplicates of the floor plan and scale cutouts for each alternate layout you want to consider. After taping all the cutouts in place, line up the alternatives and choose the one that offers the best solution to your office needs.

Simulating the layout. To double-check your decision or to decide between two or more possible layouts, give your plan a dress rehearsal. In the actual space that you've designated for your home office, simulate the proposed layout—or layouts—using string, masking tape, and cartons or lightweight pieces of furniture.

Now put yourself into the picture. Sit where you expect to sit behind your desk; walk through the routine motions of a typical workday, such as going to a supply cabinet or copier; swing around, as you would in your office chair, to work at your keyboard or talk on the phone; go to the door to meet visitors. Do these actions proceed smoothly in your proposed layout? Now is the time to refine any awkward points.

(continued on page 56)

...designing your office

U-shaped Layout

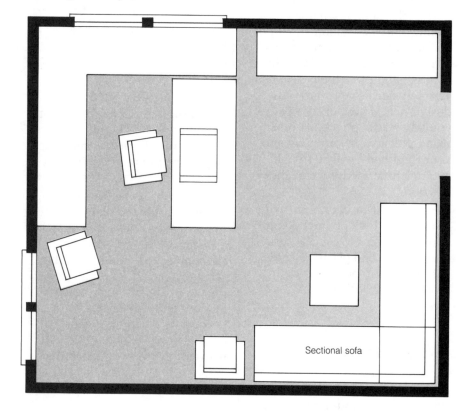

In this spacious family room, there's plenty of floor space for a compact home office. The U-shaped layout allows for convenient access to work surfaces on three sides with just a swivel of the desk chair. There's also lots of usable countertop space. Another advantage of the plan is that it separates the office area from the rest of the family room, yet does not isolate the user from contact with the family.

Straight-line Layout

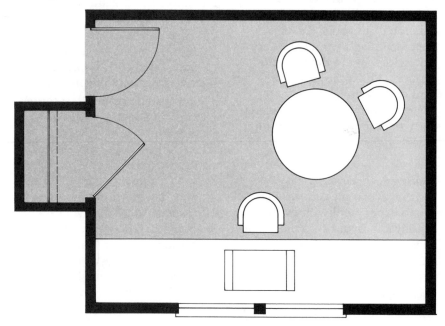

In this spare room, an office has been arranged in a straight-line layout. Running a counter down one long wall (the monotony is relieved by a window in the center) leaves ample space for a round conference table and comfortable chairs in one corner of the moderately sized room. The room's closet, at left, provides inconspicuous, built-in storage for supplies.

SAMPLE FLOOR PLAN C:
Parallel Layout

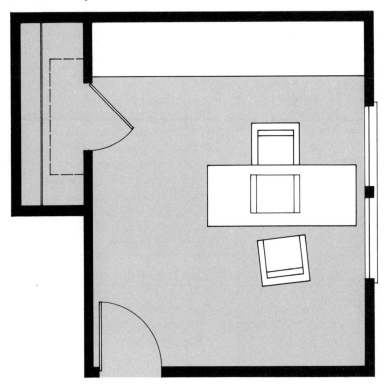

The parallel plan shown here is a popular layout for people who prefer to meet with clients across a desktop rather than around a table. Much can be stored on the counter that runs behind and parallel to the desk, leaving the desktop uncluttered. Yet everything is within easy reach.

SAMPLE FLOOR PLAN D:
L-shaped Layout

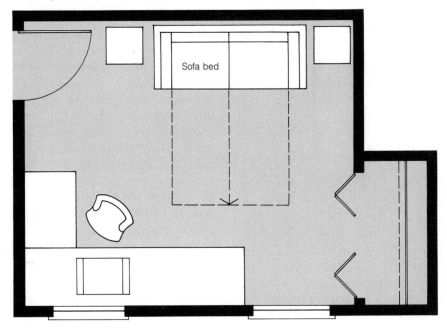

Sofa bed

An office that shares space with a guest room takes advantage of an L-shaped layout in this plan. Using a sofabed economizes space on one side of the room; a desktop that wraps around the corner maximizes the space that's left.

...designing your office

Drawing Final Plans

After you've decided on the most practical and comfortable office layout, the next step is to transfer this layout to your floor plan and elevation drawings.

Final floor plan. The preliminary floor plan, to which you have now taped scale cutouts in the final layout of the office, is a model for the final one. Use a fresh sheet of graph paper with a grid identical to that of the preliminary plan.

Counting each square carefully, transfer the office outline from the preliminary drawing to the new sheet of graph paper. Align the two drawings from time to time to double-check accuracy.

As before, draw straight horizontal lines with a T-square or ruler and right angles or vertical lines with a triangle, placing one edge over the horizontal line. Mark the location of windows, doors, and any other apertures. Set a compass to the scale of the door's width and draw its swing.

Use the architectural symbols shown on page 52 to indicate where electrical lines enter the room (also gas lines, if the room has a gas heater). Show the location of light switches, fixtures, and electrical outlets. On the final floor plan, also note which switch operates which light source and indicate whether it's a one-way or multiple switch.

To complete the final floor plan, transfer an outline of each scale cutout as arranged in the final layout of your preliminary plan. Duplicate its exact position along with its size and shape, using the same grid pattern.

Final elevations. More than the floor plan, elevation drawings can give you a preview of how furnishings, shelves, and cabinets will fit together against a wall.

For the scale cutouts used on the floor plan, you measured the width and depth (or back-to-front dimensions) of each piece of furniture or equipment, but you didn't need to know the height. For the elevation, you need to know both height and width but not depth. If you have not yet measured the height of furniture and other pieces, do so now. Mark the height and width on sketches of the appropriate pieces on a separate sheet of paper.

Working with each preliminary elevation in turn, add the scale elevations (width and height) of the office furnishings and equipment according to the layout you have chosen. Make sure that the arrangement still looks workable from the straight-on perspective. Notice whether furniture blocks any outlets and switches to which you'll need access.

Completing the drawings. To make your final floor plan and elevations even harder working, record on them as much information as possible about the office space and its fittings.

Write down the dimensions of walls, windows, doors, closets, furniture, and equipment. On outlines of furniture and equipment, write the manufacturer's name along with the model name and number.

Annotated with as much pertinent information as possible, the final floor plan and elevations become concise, portable records of your office-in-the-making.

Positioning Office Elements

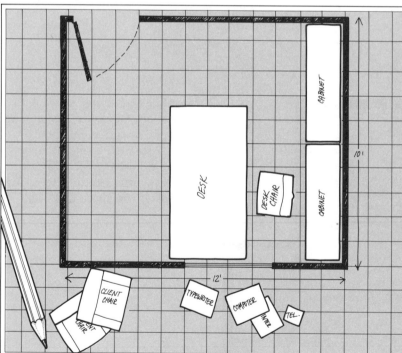

Like a puzzle, *an office layout takes shape as you piece together an arrangement that fits your space and working needs. Cut out scale models of the major elements; then, moving the cutouts around on your floor plan, experiment with various layouts.*

The Finishing Touches

After the carpenters and electricians have departed, the last of the sawdust has been vacuumed away, and your new furniture has arrived, your home office is ready for the finishing details.

Just as specialists bring their building skills to the necessary structural work, interior designers and office designers can apply their expertise to this final step. Or you can handle the decorating and finishing work yourself.

More than anything else, the finishing touches determine the face your office will present to the world. These details include types of lighting, color choices, and coverings for floors, walls, and windows.

Though the finishing touches comprise the last phase of office planning, they're no less significant to the ultimate success of your plan than the work that preceded them. How well you light your workspace, what colors set its mood, and what textures surround you all produce a subtle yet emphatic effect on you, your clients, and your work.

Lighting

The illumination that makes any room comfortable and useful comes from three different types of light. *Natural light* (or daylight) floods into a room through windows and skylights. Depending on their orientation, the time of day, the season, and the weather, natural light can have either a gentle or harsh effect on a room. Window coverings, discussed on page 61, can do much to control the harshness.

The other two kinds of light are artificial. When artificial light from a central source diffuses throughout a room and provides a uniform level of illumination, the effect is called *ambient lighting*. Artificial light that is concentrated and focused directly on a particular area is called *task lighting*. Whether or not an office benefits from natural light, it will need both types of artificial light.

Ambient lighting. Creating diffuse, soft illumination, ambient lighting for a home office requires careful planning. It's important to avoid high contrast between your work area and its surroundings. If you're working at a dark computer screen, for example, too much background light will require your eyes to adjust frequently between the dark screen and the brightly lit room. A dimmer switch is one way of controlling ambient lighting and adding flexibility to your lighting system.

If you set up a home office in an existing spare room, fixtures for ambient lighting may already be in place. If you're using part of a room, the general illumination from the adjacent shared area may adequately serve your office area. Otherwise, you'll need to add ambient lighting.

Several light sources are preferable to just one—again, the goal is flexibility. In addition to ceiling fixtures, consider table lamps, spotlights, track lighting, wall lights, and wall wash (light directed upward).

Task lighting. Whether emitted from individual table or desk lamps or from track lights mounted on the ceiling or a wall, task lighting directs a pool of illumination on areas where vision will be concentrated. A reading lamp is a good example, as are the lamps designed specifically for study and office work (see page 50).

Determining the proper amount of task lighting is central to planning an office, since office work usually involves intense, concentrated vision over many hours. Insufficient lighting can quickly lead to eye strain.

Besides inadequate lighting, glare must also be assiduously avoided. Operators of computers know how glare detracts from the visibility of a monitor screen. (For ways to control screen glare, see page 38.) Lamps should not be placed so close to a book or other work material that the light causes glare as it reflects off the paper.

If you're right-handed, task lighting should shine over your left shoulder so that your writing hand won't cast shadows on your work. If you're left-handed, it should shine over your right shoulder. Keep in mind, too, that a desk lamp with a fluorescent bulb will not cast a shadow like that of a lamp with an incandescent bulb.

Lumens and bulbs. How much lighting is enough for various kinds of work? Before you can answer this question, you'll have to weigh the following factors: (1) the visual demands of the task to be performed, (2) the speed and accuracy with which it must be completed, (3) the color contrasts among the materials involved in the task, and (4) the eyesight of the worker. In general, the more visually taxing the work, the more light should be shed on the work area.

The amount of light produced by a bulb is measured in lumens. Lumens and wattage are listed on a bulb's sleeve (see also the chart below). Lumen output diminishes with the bulb's age and can vary from one manufacturer to another.

Lumen Output of Standard Household Bulbs & Tubes

Incandescent

Watts	Lumens
25	235
40	455
60	870
75	1190
100	1750
150	2880
50/100/150	580/1670/2250

Fluorescent

Watts	Lumens
20	820
40	2150
40 (U-shaped)	1980
22 (circular)	800
40 (circular)	1900

As a rule of thumb, the most visually demanding tasks require a total of at least 2500 lumens in an average room. Part of the total should be ambient light, but the greatest number of lumens should be concentrated in task lighting. By contrast, a casual demand on the eyes, such as when you're watching television, requires only about 1500 to 2000 lumens.

To find out how many lumens are available in your office, add up the lumen output of each of the bulbs in use. For task lighting alone, determine the total lumens

Office Lighting

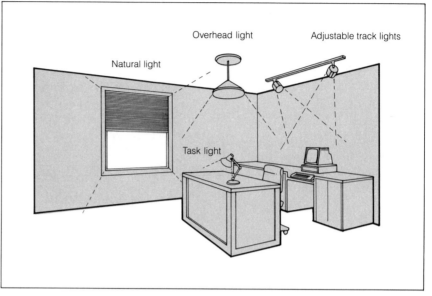

Plenty of light, *correctly directed, relieves eye strain and brightens surroundings. Here, natural light flows from a window, ambient light from a large, overhead fixture, and task lighting from the desk lamp and adjustable track fixtures.*

of the bulbs that directly illuminate your work area.

Before you choose a specific desk lamp for your office, make sure that its maximum bulb wattage will allow sufficient lumens for all the types of work you'll be performing.

Incandescent vs. fluorescent. Fluorescent bulbs usually last longer, generate less heat, and are more efficient (providing more light from less energy) than incandescent bulbs. Because the light comes evenly from the whole surface of the tube, it spreads in all directions, providing steady illumination.

On the other hand, incandescent bulbs have a warmer look and can be controlled with dimmers. And you'll have a much larger choice of styles in lamps and fixtures than with fluorescent bulbs.

A Selection of Light Bulbs

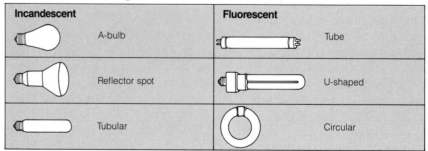

Incandescent or fluorescent? *Each type of bulb has its advantages. Study the light qualities of each and determine your preference before purchasing a desk lamp.*

In designing your office lighting, you may want to consider a combination of both types of bulbs. With careful planning, you'll be able to achieve just the lighting effects you need.

Decorating Your Office

From computer hardware to leather briefcases, many business accoutrements have a uniform look. But in your home office, you can distinctively express your own tastes and individuality.

One of the benefits of working at home is that you can choose your own colors, fabrics, and materials, and your own decorative touches. You can surround yourself with whatever style pleases you—just as you would, without thinking twice, if you were decorating the kitchen or master bedroom.

But having an office at home also makes you responsible for more than style. You need to consider office upkeep, safety, and general durability. In addition to the fun of selecting your favorite colors, you'll have to come to terms with materials and costs.

Choosing your style. Before you begin pondering such practical questions as the relative strength of various kinds of carpeting, take plenty of time to develop a sure sense of the style you want for your office.

Determining your style preferences may take some time. Start with the color photographs on pages 4–31 and 64–79 of this book. Look carefully at the rooms that please you the most, then try to analyze what it is about the style that you like. Take some notes about colors and fabrics, and supplement them with pictures you've clipped from magazines, catalogs, and advertising supplements.

If possible, visit decorators' showrooms and furniture stores. Try to find out specific names of products, interior designers, and other sources for the ideas you'd like to use.

Deciding on colors. The colors traditionally used in office decoration have been muted ones. With the exception of certain creative fields, the business world apparently runs more smoothly in an environment of calm, soothing tones, such as beiges and grays.

Look around the other rooms of your house to help you decide on the colors you can work with most comfortably. Whether you favor earth tones, crayon colors, soft pastels, bold contrasts, or delicate harmony, you can probably carry a similar theme into your office. You may notice that certain rooms have a more relaxed ambience, while others, decorated in more lively colors, are more active in feeling. Since an office should provide a relaxed environment that also stimulates energy, a balance between quiet and more vibrant colors is usually called for.

Remember, too, that color is mercurial, looking subtly or sharply different as surroundings change. Variations in light, for example, can make a great difference in the appearance of colors. You would probably choose different shades of blue for your office depending on whether the predominant daylight was sunny or overcast.

The type of light bulbs you choose can also change how colors look. A cool white fluorescent bulb will enrich and brighten greens but tone down reds. An incandescent bulb will warm up reds and cool down blues.

Deep or bright colors can make a small room seem smaller. White or a very pale color can lend a small room the illusion of greater size.

According to psychologists, color has the ability to affect our moods, as well. It has been shown that yellow inspires happiness, red kindles energy (or anger), green refreshes, and blue pacifies. Of course, color's effects on mood vary from one individual to another.

Obviously, color is a complex and personal consideration in decorating a home office. It can also provide hours of fun—and perhaps frustration—as you bring home paint, fabric, and carpet samples to try out. Proceed with caution. Keep in mind that bright, strong colors generally look best as accents—the base of a lamp, a cushion, or a picture on the wall. In broader sweeps, such as to cover the walls or the floor, quieter shades create an environment that's more comfortable for most people to work in.

For information on the color wheel and how it can help you select a pleasing color palette for your home office, be sure to read "Choosing Colors" on page 60.

Floor coverings. Though rarely noticed consciously, the floor covering often sets the mood of a room by virtue of its design, texture, and color. A wide range of materials is available, including wood, resilient vinyl and rubber, ceramic tile, masonry, and carpeting. Not all serve a home office equally well; the more you can narrow down the choices before you shop, the easier your final decision will be.

The following guidelines will help you in choosing a practical office floor covering.

- *Noise.* The right floor covering can help soundproof an office, often an important consideration. Your best bet is to choose a soft material that absorbs sound, such as vinyl, rubber, or carpeting.

...the finishing touches

- *Wear.* Though an office usually gets less traffic than many other areas of the house, you'll probably want to invest in a floor covering that will last for many years. Industrial- or commercial-grade carpeting, level loop carpeting, or studded or ribbed synthetic rubber flooring are good choices. All are available in attractive colors and styles.

- *Comfort.* If your work requires you to be on your feet for long periods of time, comfort should be a high priority item. Most comfortable underfoot are soft and resilient floor coverings—carpeting, wood, rubber, and vinyl.

- *Maintenance.* Care of a wood floor involves more fuss than care of most resilient floor coverings or carpeting. When you're choosing a floor-covering material, consider the amount of maintenance it will require.

Besides these purely practical considerations, other specific office needs should guide your choice. For example, under and around a computer, you may want to use industrial rubber tiles, which will prevent static. Or, if you plan to hold conferences in your office, an inviting plush carpet may be the most suitable choice.

The kind of work you do can also be an important determinant. If your job involves the use of chemicals or other liquids, for example, you'll want a flooring that cleans up quickly and easily, such as tile or resilient vinyl.

Wallcoverings. As with floor coverings, wallcoverings come in a broad range of styles and a wide variety of materials. In selecting one for your home office, you'll need to balance esthetics with practicality.

You can paint the walls in a solid color or in a design, or you can use wallpaper, which offers a kaleidoscope of colors, textures, and patterns.

Another option is wood paneling. It creates a cozy, warm atmosphere in the tradition of a den or study. But beware of using dark wood in a dimly lit room—the effect will be to make the room darker still.

You can buy wood paneling milled from either hardwoods (such as birch, cherry, mahogany,

Choosing Colors

The color wheel can help you choose compatible hues for your home office palette. Red, yellow, and blue are the primary colors; all other colors are formed from various mixtures of these three.

Colors that face each other across the color wheel, such as yellow and violet, are called complementary. Placed together, they create a strong contrast that's exciting to some tastes, disturbing to others. Harmonious colors, on the other hand, represent a continuous segment of the color wheel. They produce a gentle color gradation—blue to blue violet to violet, for example.

Warm colors are located around orange on the color wheel; cool ones cluster around blue. Any color can vary in value, becoming more pastel with the addition of white, or deeper with the addition of black.

Black and white are not colors, but, along with gray (a mixture of the two), they provide striking contrasts for colors. One reason for the popularity of white walls and furnishings is that white shows off colorful accents vividly.

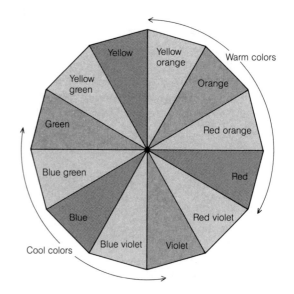

Window Covering Choices

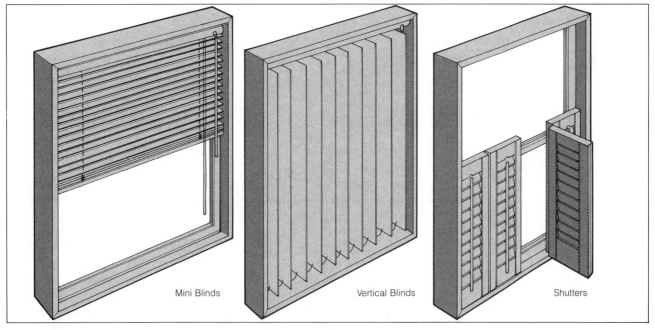

Mini Blinds

Vertical Blinds

Shutters

Tailored treatments *such as these make practical choices for office windows. At left are narrow blinds, available in many colors; at center are vertical blinds; hinged wood shutters appear at right. All three are adjustable for light control.*

and maple) or softwoods (such as cedar, fir, pine, and redwood). Another popular option is barnwood, which is composed of naturally or artificially weathered redwood or cedar. Less expensive paneling is made from a simulated wood surface applied to a wood fiber core.

Sometimes, the right wallcovering can assist you in your work. Walls of cork double as bulletin boards and offer the additional advantage of muffling sound.

Be sure to consider how various wallcoverings will coordinate with the other elements in your office. For example, if you have several large pieces of wood furniture, you many not want to cover the walls with wood paneling. Or, if you intend to hang artwork, you may want to choose a quiet coat of paint as a backdrop, rather than printed wallpaper.

Window coverings. If you're lucky enough to have a window with a pleasant view in your

office, think carefully before you add a covering. If privacy isn't a problem, you may want to leave the window uncovered.

But ensuring privacy is just one of several reasons for installing window coverings. The need to control natural light may be an even greater problem. At certain times of day, intensive, angled sunlight can become an office nuisance—even making work temporarily impossible. The right window covering can temper such interference, however.

Another common reason for putting up window coverings is for decoration. Some windows just don't look finished without some kind of treatment.

Perhaps most familiar to us are soft window coverings—curtains and drapes, or shades made of canvas or fabric. Though attractive in domestic interiors, such styles don't always serve a home office as well as such hard window coverings as blinds and shutters. Soft curtains and drapes may clut-

ter an office, especially if they have lots of folds and frills. Fabric shades, though less intrusive, allow little flexibility. Rolled up, they may let in too much light; pulled down, they block it completely.

Hard window coverings, such as the adjustable blinds and louvered shutters illustrated above, offer the greatest control over both privacy and sunlight. These window treatments stay neatly in place and provide a more tailored look to your office. Attached close to the glass and designed to blend into their surroundings rather than attract notice, blinds and shutters also intrude less upon the office and its activities.

Photographed in color, attractive examples of blinds, shutters, and other office window treatments (including none at all) appear throughout these chapters: "Finding a Space to Work" (pages 4–31) and "Tailoring Your Workspace" (pages 64–79).

Working with Professionals

From idea to fully outfitted reality, creating an office in your home can be a complex and demanding job. Even planning a computer work center in one corner of a guest bedroom can entail numerous decisions and many hours of hard work.

If your home office plans call for remodeling part of your house, popping out a wall, renovating an attic, or adding a completely new room, you'll probably want to seek the help of one or more professionals. Certain kinds of work, such as upgrading an electrical system to accommodate a computer or other equipment, require professional assistance. And professionals are available to help you plan color schemes or spatial organization, if you're unsure about making these decisions yourself.

Only you can determine whether or not you need to hire a professional. Base your decision not only on the type of work involved but also on your own abilities, the time you have available for the project, and your budget.

Choosing a Professional

Depending on the kind of help you need, professionals who might help you produce your home office include interior designers, office designers, architects, building designers, contractors, and subcontractors.

The best way to find competent assistance is to ask friends and neighbors to recommend professionals they have used. You can also seek referrals from retail building materials outlets (listed in the Yellow Pages under "Hardware" and "Lumber").

The Yellow Pages list design professionals under "Interior Decorators and Designers," "Architects," "Building Designers," and "Drafting Services"; look for contractors to handle a remodeling project under "Contractors—Alteration" and contractors for major projects such as room additions, under "Contractors—Building, General." The Yellow Pages are also a good source for more specialized assistance.

Once you've collected several names, describe your project to each person and ask to see photos or plans of their recent work. Then ask for references and call and visit home offices or other similar projects they've worked on. Observe each professional's creative approach, workmanship, and detailing.

Keep in mind that whatever changes occur with the addition of a home office will affect everyone in your family. In choosing a professional, look for someone who is not only technically and artistically skilled but also willing to accommodate your family's needs. Admittedly, it's difficult to know in advance how well any professional will work with you, but it will help if you discuss the working relationship along with technical matters at your first interview.

When you find several people you like, get bids from all of them so you can compare costs.

Whenever you consult with a professional you've hired, try to be as precise as possible about what you want. Describe the materials, furniture, and equipment you'd like to use. Collect pertinent photos from books, magazines, manufacturers' brochures, and advertisements. Also, be sure to provide your final floor plan and elevations (see page 56), as well as an idea of your budget. Write down any questions or concerns you may have in advance of the meeting. The more specific information you supply, the better the professional can serve your needs.

Interior Designers & Office Designers

Interior designers specialize in decorating and furnishing rooms. They can offer fresh, innovative ideas and advice as well as access to materials and products that you otherwise might not know about or that are available only in the wholesale market.

Though office designers more commonly plan large, commercial spaces, their expertise can also be invaluable in planning space, smooth work flow, and organized storage for a home office. Like interior designers, office designers have access to the latest in office materials and products.

Architects & Building Designers

Generally, an architect or building designer is called in only if the project involves remodeling or new construction. Either professional can draw plans acceptable to building department officials.

Other duties performed by architects and building designers include specifying materials for a contractor to order, sending out bids, helping you select a contractor, and supervising the contractor's performance according to plan and schedule. Some architects and building designers even act as their own contractors.

The difference between architects and building designers is that most states do not require designers to be licensed, as architects must be. For this reason, designers often charge lower fees than architects. However, if stress calculations need to be made, a designer has to hire a state-licensed engineer to design the structure; an architect can make the necessary calculations alone.

Architects and building designers sometimes charge for time spent in an exploratory interview. Most charge on an hourly basis for drawing plans. For selecting and supervising a contractor, they're paid either an hourly rate or a percentage (typically 25 percent) of the cost of materials and labor. Make sure that all charges and descriptions of services are stated and agreed to in advance to prevent misunderstandings later on.

For a project as small as a home office, you may be able to entice an apprentice or drafter who works in an architect's office to draw up your plans. Such services are normally paid for on an hourly basis.

Contractors

Besides performing construction tasks, contractors can often draw expert plans acceptable to building department officials. They can also obtain all necessary building permits and apply their experience and know-how to many aspects of your project. Like an architect or building designer, a contractor is helpful only for home office projects that involve construction. If you plan to pop out a wall or remodel your home to create office space, you'll probably require the services of a contractor.

Contact at least three state-licensed contractors and give each one either plans and specifications prepared by an architect or designer, or an exact description and sketches of the work you want done. Include a detailed account of who will be responsible for what work.

In comparing bids, also consider reliability, quality of work, and on-time performance. Ask each contractor for references and follow up by calling several of them to check on satisfaction. If possible, go to see work they've done.

To be sure of the contractor's financial responsibility, check bank and credit references. Your local Better Business Bureau can tell you about any complaints they've received.

Most contractors bid a fixed fee for remodeling, to be paid in installments based on the amount of work completed. Most states limit the amount of "good faith" money that a contractor can require in advance of starting work. Though some contractors base their fee on a percentage of materials and labor costs, choosing a fixed-fee bid protects you against any unexpected rise in prices.

After you decide on a contractor, make sure your written agreement includes the following: plans and materials specifications, services to be supplied, costs plus method and schedule of payment, time schedule, and warranty against defects. Not only does the contract bind both parties to the agreement, but it also minimizes future problems by clearly defining responsibilities.

Try to make your plans as specific and complete as possible before starting construction. Changes made during construction can be costly and can involve considerable delays.

Subcontractors & Other Workers

If you have the time and expertise, you can act as your own general contractor and put parts of your project out to bid with subcontractors (such as electricians or cabinetmakers). If so, you must use the same care in hiring subcontractors as you would in hiring a general contractor. Once you've received bids, work out a detailed contract for each specific job, and carefully supervise the work.

You may also want to hire workers on an hourly basis for their specialized skills. If you hire such help, you may have to provide workers' compensation insurance to cover possible job-related injuries.

Though provisions vary from state to state, compensation insurance usually reimburses the injured worker for lost wages and for the cost of medical treatment. Workers' compensation policies are available from insurance companies.

If you employ people directly and they earn more than a minimum amount set by the state, you must register with the state and federal governments as an employer. You'll be required to withhold and remit state and federal income taxes; withhold, remit, and contribute to Social Security; and pay state unemployment insurance. For information, talk to an official from your local building department or look under the subheading "Taxes" listed under your state in the telephone directory.

Tailoring Your Workspace

Once you've found suitable home office space—whether an entire room or a smaller area—you can turn your thoughts to the satisfying project of tailoring it to meet your needs.

The term "tailoring" fits a well-designed work environment as smoothly as it does a business suit. It implies quality of materials and workmanship, as well as attention to detail.

Of course, much of the stitching that shapes a well-cut jacket is hidden behind lining or seams, so the wearer may have no idea it's there at all. Similarly, in a well-tailored office space, a visitor would have no idea that the richly textured wall covering deadens sound, the stylish Italian rubber flooring eliminates static, or the posh armchairs promote correct posture. Tailoring produces a design that incorporates all these practical functions smoothly, in one unified and visually pleasing scheme.

Exactly where items are placed is also determined by adroit office tailoring. In addition to producing attractive surroundings, the intent is always to assure physical comfort, maximum accessibility of equipment, and client ease and confidence.

In this chapter, you'll see many examples of home office elements that coordinate smoothly in workspaces that are at once comfortable and efficient, energetic yet calm. Because a desk or other work surface is usually the hub of most home office activity, we open the chapter with a look at a wide range of designs for desks and computer work centers. You'll see that it's possible to choose a desk style suited to your own work needs, space limitations, and personal taste.

Moving out from the desk, the remainder of the chapter displays attractive ways to resolve some of the spatial problems of home office tailoring—handling storage needs smoothly and working out the best shared-office arrangements.

Hopefully, each of the photos will include one or more ideas that you can use in tailoring your own home workspace.

A state of mind *as well as a room in the house, a home office requires many design decisions—involving wall color, woodwork, and carpeting, for example—to achieve the right fit. Architect: David S. Gast.*

Work Surfaces

CHOOSING A DESK

Computer Chic
Putting a corner to practical use, this L-shaped modular system caters to every computer and office need. At center, opened drawer reveals a printer. Counter widens slightly to accommodate a desktop copying machine. Furniture design: Eurodesign, Ltd.

Design-a-desk

Like a child's construction toy, this amazing oak desk tilts, lifts, or lowers as you adjust its knob-and-pegboard frame. Furniture design: Dean Santner Designs.

Right at Home

Compact, U-shaped computer work center, available commercially, puts every office chore within a spin of the chair. Central unit holds keyboard, CPU, and monitor, while providing convenient storage for manuals and other supplies. Printer stand includes a shelf for fanfold paper. Typewriter sits atop a roll-around unit with storage beneath. Furniture design: Bush Industries, Inc.

…work surfaces

Point of View

A command post for people who like to think on their feet, this stand-up desk also affords a panoramic view of surrounding hills. Close at hand is an oversize plastic-coated note board (its colorful jottings wipe off easily). Interior design: Sally Champe.

A Place for Everything

An elegant, contemporary design, this desk employs a feature favored in the past—pigeonholes. Collecting letters, business cards, and other small essentials, they clear the desk for the day's work. Furniture design: Williams & Foltz.

Updated Classic

The classic rolltop enters the computer age in this handsome oak version. Recessed in their own compartments, the monitor and CPU sit within easy view and reach. The keyboard and printer slide out when needed. Furniture design: Windsor.

...work surfaces

Antique Appeal

Once beckoning Britons to breakfast, this antique hunt table now entices family members to sample the contents of the library shelves. Architect: Sigrid Rupp.

Library Table

The nature of work varies widely, and so does the purpose of a desk. In this studious retreat, it supports one heavy book—rather than the more expected clutter of papers, pens, and telephone. Architect: David S. Gast.

Putting Walls to Work

SHELVING VARIATIONS

High Brackets

Held secure by pressure devices, the freestanding uprights on these bookcases allow the brackets to face the walls. In turn, the brackets bear laden shelves stacked all the way to the ceiling. Design: Mara Jones.

Boxed In

Recessed between wall studs, these shelves form a pattern of squares. Books and supplies enliven the orderly cubicles with varied forms and colors. Architect: Richard N. Pollack.

…putting walls to work

Scholastic Prize

Acquired from Harvard University, these bookcases protect their printed freight with glass fronts that swing up and slide back to make the volumes available. An old law school tradition, their design brings distinction today to the home office of a CPA.

Parade of Print

*For many people, reading magazines is a form of relaxation. But for the free-lance writer who owns this home office, all those periodicals provide a stock-in-trade. The wide, tilted shelf below the bookcase allows their vivid display.
Design: Peter Van Dyke and Tim Cook.*

Open & Shut Case

Bleached pine cabinets encase books and a computer work area along one wall of this study. Hinged doors fold out of the way for access—then shut to keep contents hidden from view. Interior design: Interior Design Works, Ltd.

Behind Closed Drawers

STYLISH FILES

Objets d'Art

Architects and graphic designers rely on flat files for protective storage of blueprints and art boards. The built-in example, at right, artfully reshapes a niche in the office wall. The unit shown below includes both horizontal drawers and vertical slots. Design at right: Osburn Design. Design below: Limn.

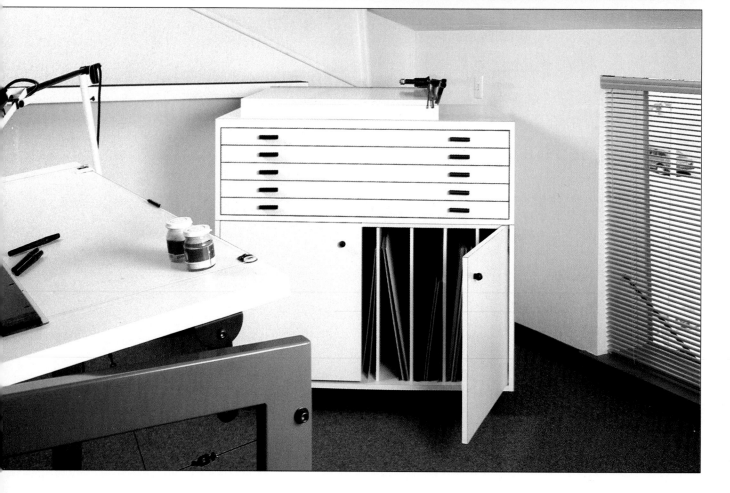

Easy Access

Delicate floppy disks require safe storage. Both of these drawers protect the floppies, yet keep them within easy reach when needed. The drawer at left features built-in compartments; the other one resembles a library index file drawer. Design at left: Eurodesign, Ltd. Design at right: Windsor.

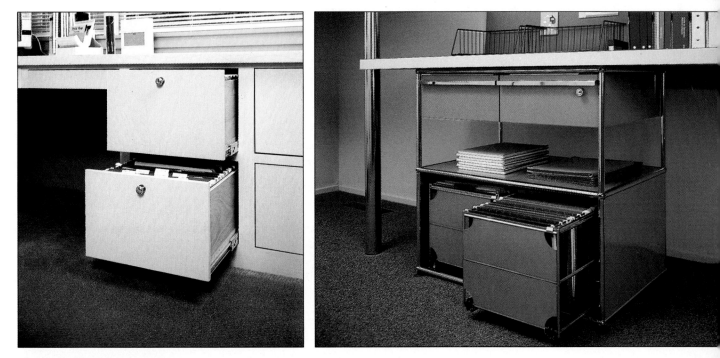

Hard-working Assistants

Businesses may sink or swim on the flow of their paper, which, in turn, often depends on the quality of its storage. Documents and correspondence that may otherwise be mislaid or fall prey to spilled coffee will stay clean and organized with filing systems such as these. Design at left: Lynn Williams of The French Connection. Design at right: Haller Systems.

Shared Office Space

FOR WORKING COUPLES

His & Hers

Staircase separates her territory on the mezzanine from his down below. Each works within easy earshot of the other, yet each stays out of sight in this semiprivate arrangement. Furniture design: Williams & Foltz.

Merger

Twin desks meet face-to-face in this shared office that occupies one end of a master bedroom. The wall system dividing the space holds work supplies on the office side, clothing on the other. Design: Ruth Soforenko Associates.

...shared office space

Their Hideaway

Wraparound cabinetwork of bleached oak establishes the warm, informal style of this spacious office, adjoining the master bedroom. In addition to comfortable work areas for husband and wife, there's room to spare for client meetings and conferences. Architect: Pierre Prodis.

Two's Company

Popular for home offices because it puts limited space to maximum use, an L-shaped layout offers a special advantage to working couples. Though close by, the two still gain privacy by sitting perpendicular to each other. The "L" also neatly divides one work area, such as the computer station shown here, from another. Interior design: Holly Hulburd.

Office Furniture You Can Make

Working in a home office allows considerably more freedom than working in most corporate settings. You can keep odd hours, dress casually, and express more individuality in your choice of office furnishings.

One way to personalize your home workspace is by building some of your own furniture and accessories. In this chapter we present seven distinctive projects, each accompanied by clear, step-by-step directions and detailed drawings.

Our first project is a basic one— a sturdy computer table that's large enough for your PC, plus a printer and accessories.

The next three projects are designed for efficiency. The desk-top organizer re-creates, in contemporary style, the cubbyholes of a classic rolltop desk. The copy/floppy holder does double duty, holding copy on top and storing floppy disks safely within. And our portable printer stand will keep your output moving right along.

Another handy office furnishing is our roll-around file, designed to hold both letter- and legal-size file folders. Small enough to fit under your desk, it travels out on casters when needed.

The designer or artist will appreciate our sleek drafting table. You can adjust its top to provide either a flat or angled work surface.

The last project is wall-hung shelves, which make a handsome cache for your books and manuals. You can tailor the dimensions and construction of these shelves to your own needs and skill.

These projects were designed as a group—all will function compatibly in one office space. But you don't have to make them all; even just one or two pieces will enhance your home working environment.

A few of the projects can be built with hand tools alone; most, however, require a combination of hand and power tools. Though a radial-arm or table saw would make all projects easier, you can successfully build them using a portable circular saw and a router.

A partnership *of wood, tools, designs, and skill can produce elegant furniture and accessories for any home office.*

Computer Table

Large enough to hold a personal computer, printer, and accessories, yet small enough to fit in even a compact office, this computer table combines efficiency with simplicity of construction. For even greater versatility, add the desktop organizer that appears on page 85.

If you need greater depth than butcher block's 25-inch width allows, you can make your own laminated top by edge-gluing 1½-inch-thick lumber up to 30 inches wide, then centering the top on the frame.

1. If you've bought rough lumber, surface it (or have it surfaced) to 1½-inch and ¾-inch thicknesses, then cut all pieces to size. Cut the half-lap joints as shown in top supports **A**, bottom supports **B**, and uprights **C**, using a radial-arm or table saw with a dado blade, or a router with a straight bit. Next, cut notches in uprights **C** to receive crossbrace **D**. Cut the curved ends of top and bottom supports **A** and **B** as shown in the detail drawing.

2. Lay out all screws. First, bore countersink holes: For the 1¼-inch screws fastening uprights **C** to top and bottom supports **A** and **B**, the countersink holes must be just deep enough to allow the heads of the screws to be covered with putty; the counterbore for the 2½-inch screws holding top **E** to top supports **A** should be 1 inch deep (see detail drawing). The 2-inch screws holding crossbrace **D** to uprights **C** will use finishing washers, so they require no countersinking. After you've bored the countersink holes, drill clearance holes for all screws.

Next, do a test fitting of each end assembly. When the half-lap joints fit perfectly and the top and bottom supports are exactly parallel to each other (measure at both ends), use a scratch awl through the clearance holes in uprights **C** to lay out pilot holes in top and bottom supports **A** and **B**; then drill the pilot holes.

Do a similar test assembly of crossbrace **D** and uprights **C**. Be sure that uprights **C** are parallel, then lay out and drill the pilot holes.

3. Glue and screw uprights **C** to top and bottom supports **A** and **B**, double-checking to make sure the supports are parallel. Then glue and screw crossbrace **D** to uprights **C**, using the finishing washers.

4. Install the adjustable glides on bottom supports **B**, following the manufacturer's instructions. Fill the screw holes in the uprights with putty. Finish-sand the frame, removing all excess glue and putty, and easing all edges. Finally,

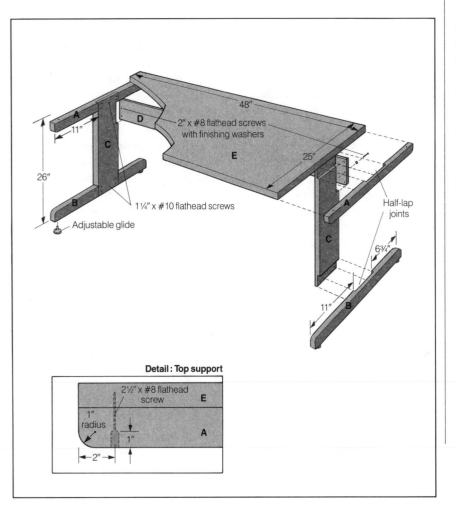

48″

D   2″ x #8 flathead screws with finishing washers

A

11″

C

26″

E

25″

B

Adjustable glide

1¼″ x #10 flathead screws

A

Half-lap joints

C

6¾″

11″

B

Detail : Top support

2½″ x #8 flathead screw

E

1″ radius

1″

A

2″

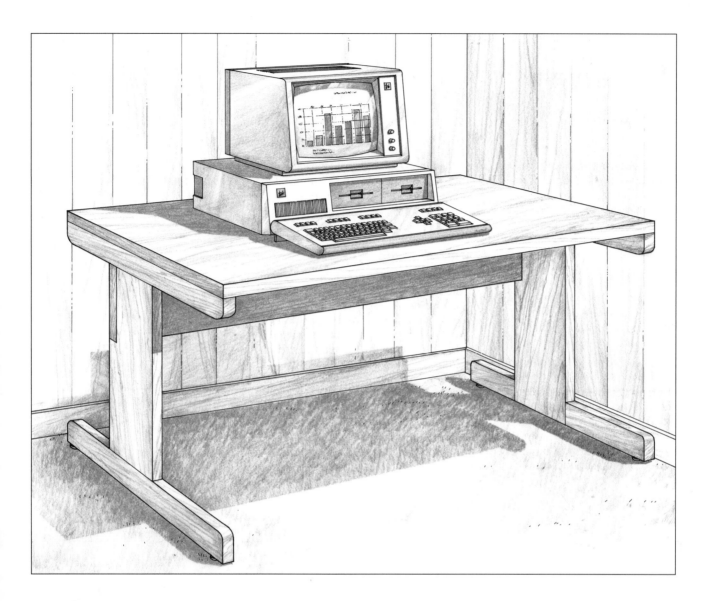

apply polyurethane penetrating oil sealer to the frame.

5. Place top **E** face down on a blanket or drop cloth and carefully position the frame, upside down, on the top. When the alignment is right (flush on all sides), mark and drill pilot holes in top **E**, then screw *but don't glue* top supports **A** to top **E**. Butcher block usually comes prefinished. If yours is, you're done. Otherwise, finish-sand and apply polyurethane penetrating oil sealer to the top.

BUY	TO MAKE	
Maple or birch		
9 ± board feet of ¾ stock	2 Top supports	A: 1½″ by 2½″ by 25″
	2 Bottom	
	supports	B: 1½″ by 2½″ by 25″
	2 Uprights	C: 1½″ by 7¼″ by 24½″
3 ± board feet of ¾ stock	1 Crossbrace	D: ¾″ by 7¼″ by 48″
Maple butcher block		
1 1½ by 25 by 48 inches	1 Top	E: 1½″ by 25″ by 48″

MISCELLANEOUS
4 adjustable glides • 4 flathead Phillips woodscrews, 2½″ by #8 • 6 flathead Phillips woodscrews, 2″ by #8, with finishing washers • 20 flathead Phillips woodscrews, 1¼″ by #10 • Wood glue • Wood putty • Polyurethane penetrating oil sealer

Desktop Organizer

Clear the clutter from your workspace with this simple desktop organizer. The system consists of two side units with adjustable shelves and a modular center unit, the length of which can be customized to fit the width of virtually any desk.

Construction is simple and most of the pieces are cut from standard-dimension lumber. However, you will need a router or a radial-arm or table saw in order to cut the rabbets and dadoes.

1. Cut all pieces to size. Rabbet all sides **A** and **D** to receive top shelves **B** and **E**, and rabbet sides **D** for bottom shelf **F**. Then rabbet pieces **A**, **B**, **D**, **E**, and **F** to receive backs **H** and **I**. As you're cutting the joints, keep in mind that sides **A** and **D** must be cut in right and left pairs. Cut dadoes in sides **A** to receive bottom shelves **C**.

2. Using Detail 1, lay out the location of the shelf peg holes in sides **A** and the screw clearance holes in one "left" **A** and one "right" **A**. Drill the screw clearance holes all the way through. You won't need countersink holes for the drywall screws.

3. Assemble the cabinets with their front edges down on a flat surface. For each side unit, spread glue and clamp top shelf **B** into the rabbets and bottom shelf **C** into the dadoes in sides **A**. Clamp across the top and bottom so that you can still insert back **H**.

Spread glue sparingly for back **H** and set it in place. Make sure the unit is square and that the bottom edge of back **H** is flush with the bottom of bottom shelf **C**. Nail back **H** with 2d finishing nails spaced about 5 inches apart and set the nails slightly below the surface.

Assemble the center unit in the same way, gluing and clamping shelves **E** and **F** into sides **D**, then gluing and nailing back **I**.

4. After the glue has cured and the clamps have been removed, use a router with a chamfer bit to cut the bevels as shown in Detail 2. Bevel the outside face edges of pieces **A**, **B**, **D**, **E**, and **F**, and the top edges of sides **A** and **D**.

5. Fill the nail holes in the back with putty. Sand all the units and finish with polyurethane penetrating oil sealer.

6. Set the side units upside down, then position the center unit between them. Screw the units together through the holes, using 1¼-inch drywall screws. You won't need pilot holes.

7. Set the assembled organizer in place on your desk and add the shelf pegs and adjustable shelves **G**.

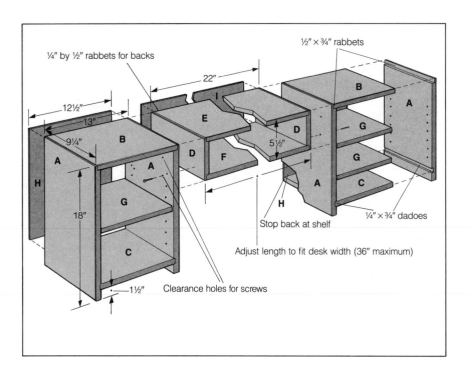

Detail 1: Drilling pattern

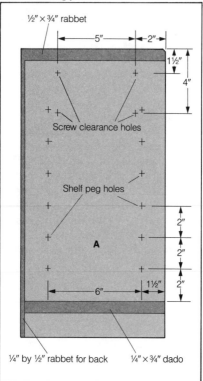

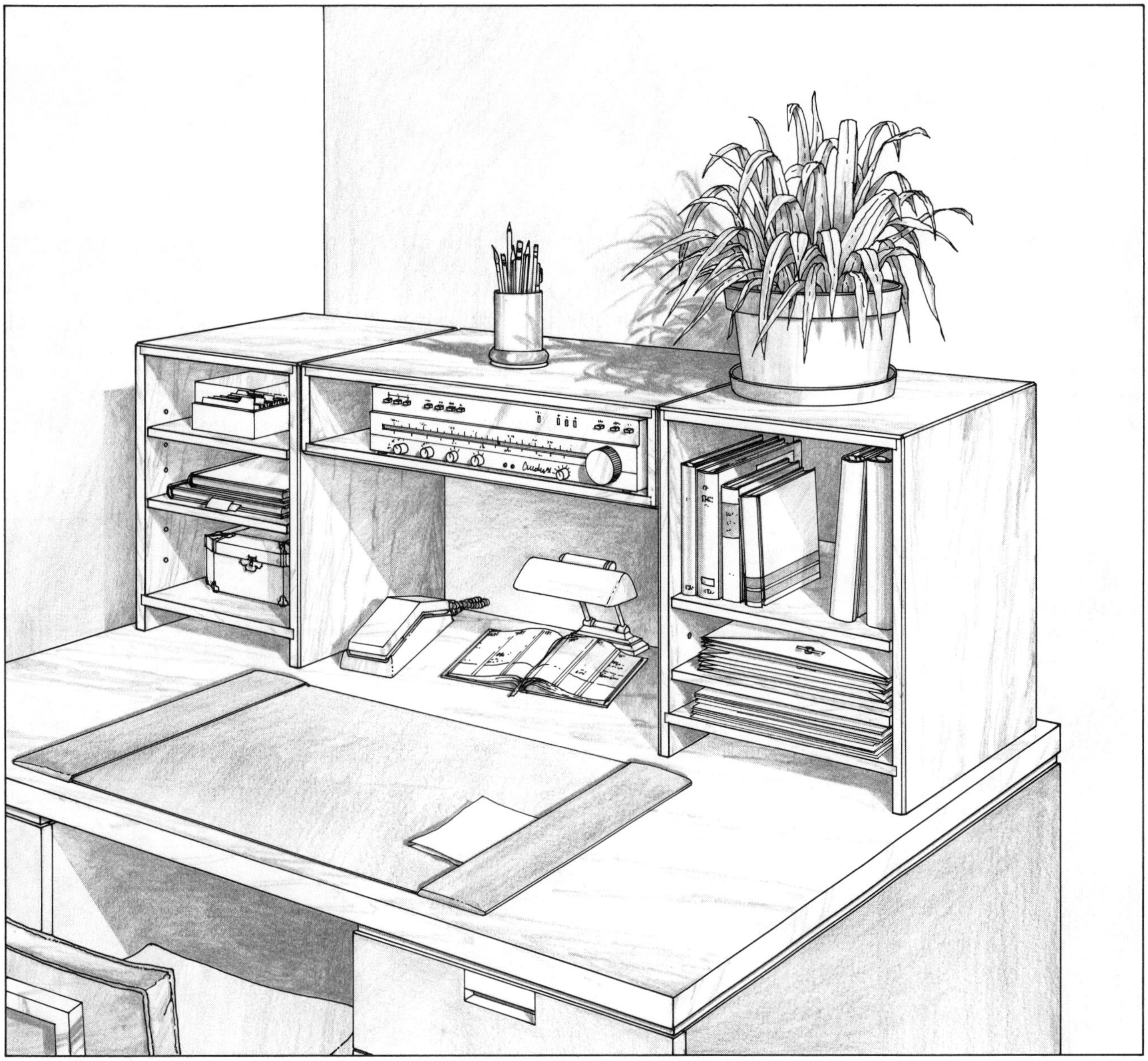

Detail 2: Bevels

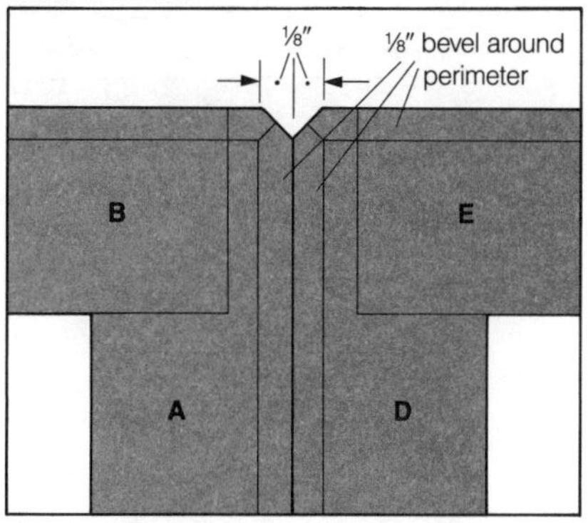

⅛″
⅛″ bevel around perimeter
B
E
A
D

BUY	TO MAKE		
Clear Douglas fir			
2 10-foot 1 by 10s	4 Sides	A:	¾″ by 9¼″ by 18″
	2 Top shelves	B:	¾″ by 9¼″ by 12½″
	2 Bottom shelves	C:	¾″ by 9″ by 12″
	2 Sides	D:	¾″ by 9¼″ by 5½″
	1 Top shelf	E:	¾″ by 9¼″ by 21½″
	1 Bottom shelf	F:	¾″ by 9¼″ by 21½″
	4 Adjustable shelves	G:	¾″ by 9″ by 11¼″
Birch plywood (shop grade)			
1 ¼-inch 2- by 4-foot piece	2 Backs	H:	12½″ by 16¼″
	1 Back	I:	5″ by 21½″

MISCELLANEOUS

16 shelf pegs • 8 drywall screws, 1¼″ by #6 • 2d finishing nails • Wood glue • Wood putty • Polyurethane penetrating oil sealer

Copy/Floppy Holder

With this handy desktop accessory, you can support the source of your ideas while you're working at your computer, then, when you're done, store the digitized rendition of your efforts in its flip-top floppy disk file. Use it in its closed position to hold anything from a single sheet of paper to a book at a handy angle for viewing; when you lift the lid, there's room for up to fifty 5¼-inch diskettes.

You'll need a router or a radial-arm or table saw to cut the rabbets and dadoes. Buy the acrylic sheet cut to size, or cut it yourself, using a carbide-tipped saw blade or router bit.

1. Lay out all pieces and cut **A**, **B**, **D**, **E**, **G**, and **H** to the dimensions shown in the materials list. Cut front **C** and back **F** to length; then set your saw to 30° and rip them to width with bevels as shown in Detail 1. Cut the ¼- by ¼-inch dadoes for bottom **H** in sides **A**, back **B**, and front **C**, and cut the dadoes for divider **D**

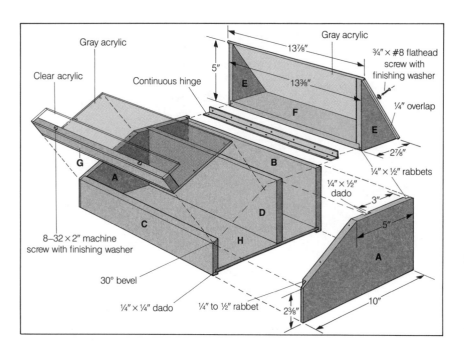

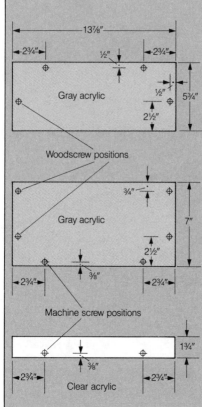

Detail 2: Acrylic layout

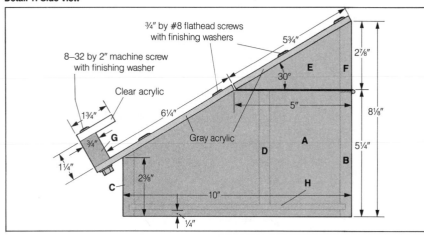

Detail 1: Side view

in sides **A**. Then rabbet sides **A** and **E** to receive front **C** and backs **B** and **F**. Finally, cut the angle sides **A** and **E** as shown in Detail 1, and double-check to make sure the angle cuts on **E** flow smoothly into the angle cuts on **A**.

2. Use Detail 2 to lay out screw clearance holes in the acrylic sheet; then clamp the acrylic to scrap wood backing, set your drill at its highest speed, and drill, feeding the bit slowly through the plastic. Use the holes in the acrylic as a layout guide, then drill clearance holes for the machine screws all the way through spacer **G**.

3. Holding bottom **H** in its dadoes, glue and clamp sides **A** to front **C** and back **B**. The top of the back should be ³⁄₁₆ inch lower than the sides to allow for the hinge. Slide divider **D** into place. Attach the clear acrylic and the spacer **G** to the large piece of gray acrylic, using machine screws as shown in Detail 1.

Set the acrylic assembly on the box so the top edge of the acrylic lines up with the top of the angle cuts on sides **A** and so the acrylic overlaps each side by ¼ inch. Using the clearance holes in the acrylic as a guide, drill pilot holes in the sides and fasten the assembly, using woodscrews and finishing washers.

Next, glue and clamp sides **E** to back **F**, and set the smaller piece of gray acrylic in place. Letting the acrylic overlap the sides by ¼ inch and keeping sides **E** carefully aligned, drill pilot holes into **E** and **F** (be sure not to drill through the back of **F**). Attach the acrylic with woodscrews and finishing washers. After tightening, recheck the alignment.

4. Screw the hinge to the upper and lower backs as shown, lining it up very carefully so its edges are flush with the front edge of both backs.

5. Finish-sand all wood surfaces, easing sharp edges slightly, then apply the clear wood finish of your choice.

BUY		TO MAKE		
Maple or other hardwood				
½-inch stock (about 6 inches by 6 feet)		2 Sides	**A:**	5¼″ by 10″
		1 Back	**B:**	5¹⁄₁₆″ by 12⅞″
		1 Front	**C:**	2¾″ by 12⅞″
		1 Divider	**D:**	4¾″ by 12⅞″
		2 Sides	**E:**	2⅞″ by 5″
		1 Back	**F:**	2⅞″ by 12⅞″
¾-inch stock		1 Spacer	**G:**	1¼″ by 13⅞″
Hardboard or plywood				
¼-inch material		1 Bottom	**H:**	9⅜″ by 12¾″

MISCELLANEOUS
¼″ gray acrylic sheet sufficient to make 1 piece at 7″ by 13⅞″, 1 piece at 5¾″ by 13⅞″ • ¼″ clear acrylic sheet sufficient to make 1 piece at 1¾″ by 13⅞″ • Continuous hinge, 1¹⁄₁₆″ by 12⅞″, with woodscrews • 8 flathead woodscrews, ¾″ by #8, with finishing washers • 2 flathead machine screws, 8-32 by 2″, with finishing washers, nuts, and washers • Wood glue • Clear wood finish

Printer Stand

This self-contained printer stand combines a number of very useful features. You can store a full box of fanfold paper on the infeed shelf, and your printout can restack several inches high on the outfeed shelf. Best of all, both shelves are easily accessible from the front of the printer stand.

Your printer will be at a convenient height to use whether you're standing or sitting, and the stand can be placed right next to a wall or desk. You can hang your fanfold paper over the dowel in back while you print on letterhead or labels, and the ribbons and other accessories can all be stored on the bottom shelf. Since the stand is on casters, it can be moved easily.

If your printer is larger than a standard 80-column size, you can increase the stand's width or depth as necessary. You can also customize it with a drawer or slide-out shelf on the bottom.

A table saw is best for cutting the plywood. Otherwise, the stand can be built with basic tools.

1. Cut all plywood pieces to size (see Detail 1). Cut the cable slots in back **G** as shown in the drawing. Shape the top

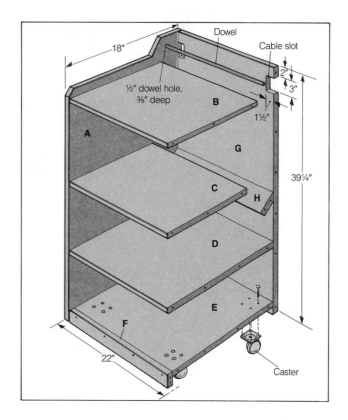

Detail 2: Bevelled edges & screw holes

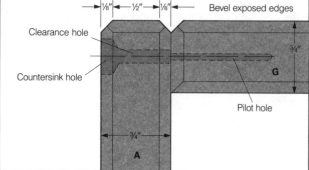

Detail 3: Layout for shelves & screws

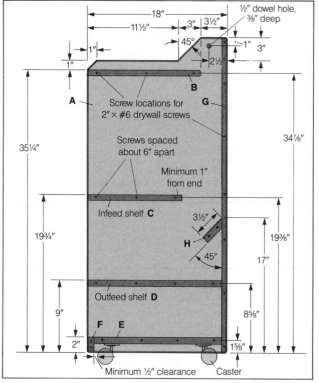

Detail 1: Plywood cutting layout

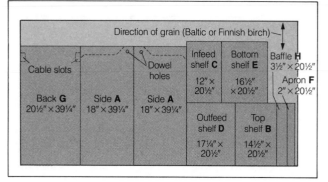

of sides **A** as shown in Detail 3, making one right and one left side that are symmetrical.

Bevel all exposed edges as shown in Detail 2; also bevel the edges of the cable slots in back **G** and the bottom back edge of top shelf **B**. A router with a chamfer bit makes clean bevels very quickly, but careful use of a hand plane or table saw could also do the job.

Lay out and drill ⅜-inch-deep dowel holes on the inside of sides **A** as shown in Detail 3. Cut the dowel to length. Cut the 45° angle on one edge of baffle **H**.

2. Lay out the position of all four shelves and baffle **H** on the inside of sides **A** as shown in Detail 3. Lay out all screw holes on the outside of sides **A** as shown in Detail 3, on apron **F** where it meets shelf **E**, and on back **G** where it meets shelves **D** and **E**; space the holes about 6 inches apart. Drill clearance, countersink, and pilot holes for all drywall screws as shown in Detail 2. The clearance holes should be just large enough so that the screws fit snugly, and the countersink holes should be just deep enough so that the heads of the screws can be covered with putty.

3. To begin assembly, glue and screw apron **F** to bottom shelf **E**. Set the assembled pieces with apron **F** face down on a flat surface. Glue and screw one side **A** to **E** and **F**. Then add shelves **B**, **C**, and **D**. Holding the dowel in place, glue and screw second side **A** to the four shelves. Now slide baffle **H** into position and screw it in place through sides **A**. Finally, glue and screw back **G** into position.

4. Lay out the casters on the corners of bottom shelf **E**, positioning each so the ball will have ½-inch clearance on all sides. Then lay out and drill ⁷⁄₃₂-inch holes through **E** for the ³⁄₁₆-inch machine screws (the slightly oversize holes will allow the flat heads to countersink themselves as you tighten the nuts). Then install the casters.

5. Fill all screw holes and any voids in the edges with putty. Sand all exposed surfaces, being careful not to round over the bevelled edges; make sure that back **G**, baffle **H**, and the bottom back edge of top shelf **B** are absolutely smooth so that paper can flow freely. Finally, apply two coats of polyurethane penetrating oil sealer or finish as desired.

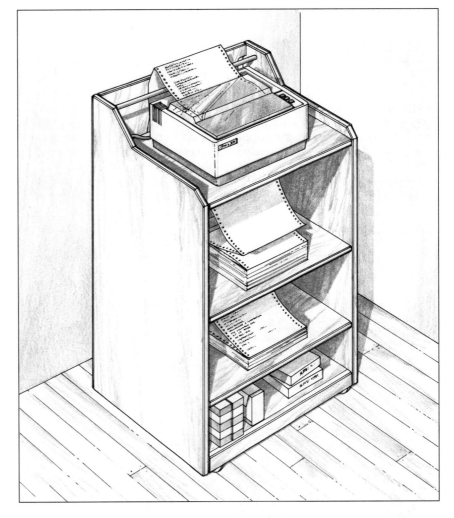

BUY	TO MAKE
Baltic or Finnish birch plywood	
1 ¾-inch 4- by 8-foot sheet	Pieces **A–H** (see Detail 1)

MISCELLANEOUS
½″ hardwood dowel sufficient to make 1 piece at 21⅛″ long • 4 plate-mounted swivel casters, 2″ diameter • 62 drywall screws, 2″ by #6 • 16 flathead machine screws, ³⁄₁₆″ by 1¼″, with nuts and washers • Wood glue • Wood putty • Polyurethane penetrating oil sealer

Tub File

Designed to accommodate letter-size hanging file folders in one section and legal-size ones in another, this handy roll-around file can be your chairside companion, yet it's short enough to slide out of the way under most desks or tables.

Baltic or Finnish birch plywood offers superior strength and good-looking edges for the file. If you plan to paint it, you can substitute shop-grade or paint-grade domestic birch plywood.

Accuracy is very important both for the strength of the file and so that the hanging file folders will slide smoothly. A table or radial-arm saw is best for cutting the plywood.

1. Cut all plywood pieces to size (see Detail 1). Bevel all exposed edges as shown in Detail 2. A router with a cham-

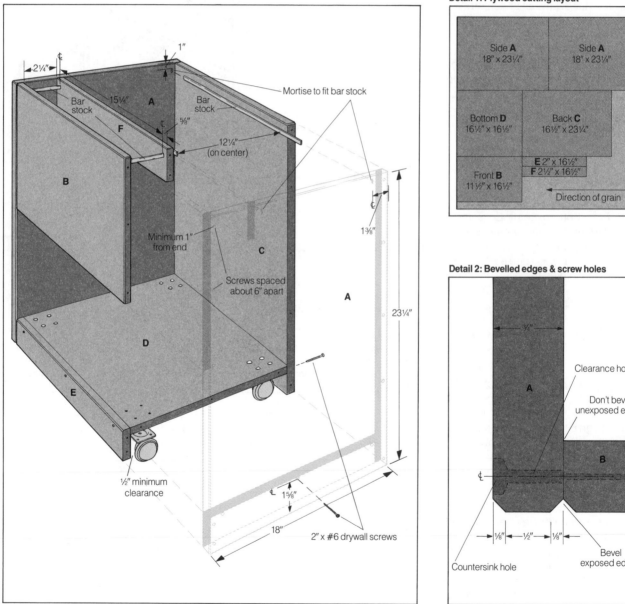

Mortise to fit bar stock

Bar stock

Bar stock

2¼"

15⅛"

1"

⅝"

A

F

B

12¼"
(on center)

Minimum 1"
from end

Screws spaced
about 6" apart

C

A

D

23¼"

E

½" minimum
clearance

1⅜"

1⅝"

18"

2" x #6 drywall screws

Detail 1: Plywood cutting layout

Side **A**
18" x 23¼"

Side **A**
18" x 23¼"

Bottom **D**
16½" x 16½"

Back **C**
16½" x 23¼"

E 2" x 16½"

Front **B**
11½" x 16½"

F 2½" x 16½"

Direction of grain

Detail 2: Bevelled edges & screw holes

¾"

A

Clearance hole

Don't bevel
unexposed edges

B

¾"

⅛" ½" ⅛"

Countersink hole

Bevel
exposed edges

fer bit makes clean bevels very quickly, but careful use of a hand plane or table saw could also do the job. Lay out and cut ¼-inch-deep mortises for the bar stock in both sides **A** and in front **B** and divider **F**. Cut the bar stock to length.

2. Lay out all screw holes, spacing them about 6 inches apart. Drill clearance, countersink, and pilot holes for all screws as shown in Detail 2. The clearance holes should be just large enough so that the screws fit snugly, and the countersink holes should be just deep enough so that the heads of the screws can be filled with putty.

3. When assembling the pieces, be careful to line up the edges accurately. You may need to clamp the pieces together or ask a friend for help while assembling. Set the screws into the clearance holes so the sharp tip just protrudes and use them to help the alignment.

Glue and screw apron **E** and back **C** to bottom **D**. Glue and screw one side **A** to the back, bottom, and apron. While holding the 16⅞-inch bar stock pieces in their mortises, attach second side **A**. Glue and screw front **B** into place through the sides. Finally, holding the 2 ⅝-inch bar stock pieces in their mortises in front **B**, glue and screw through sides **A** into divider **F**.

4. Lay out the casters on the corners of bottom **D**, positioning them so the ball will have ½-inch clearance on all sides. Then lay out and drill through **D** for the machine screws and install the casters.

5. Fill all screw holes and any voids in the edges with putty. Sand all exposed surfaces, being careful not to round over the bevelled edges. Then either finish with two coats of polyurethane penetrating oil sealer or prime and paint.

BUY	TO MAKE
Baltic or Finnish birch plywood	
1 ¾-inch 4- by 4-foot sheet	Pieces **A–F** (see Detail 1)

MISCELLANEOUS
³⁄₃₂″ by ½″ aluminum bar stock sufficient to make 2 pieces at 16⅞″ and 2 pieces at 2⅝″ • 4 plate-mounted swivel casters, 2″ diameter • 16 flathead machine screws, ³⁄₁₆″ by 1¼″, with nuts and washers • 36 drywall screws, 2″ by #6 • Wood glue • Wood putty • Polyurethane penetrating oil sealer or high-gloss enamel paint

Drafting Table

Clean lines and straightforward construction characterize this adjustable-top drafting table. Drop the top to its horizontal position and you have a flat, solid work surface; or raise the top and use the table for drafting or graphic art.

If you'll be using a T-square on your drafting table, you may want to add the aluminum sides.

1. Cut all pieces to size. Cut the half-lap joints as shown in top supports **A**, bottom supports **B**, and uprights **C**, using a radial-arm or table saw with a dado blade, or a router with a straight bit. Next, cut notches in uprights **C** to receive crossbrace **D**. Cut a 1-inch radius on the ends of bottom supports **B**. Bevel the ends of top supports **A**, then lay out and cut mortises to fit the back-flap hinges in the top supports as shown in the detail drawing. (If back-flap hinges are unavailable, substitute 1½-inch butt hinges.)

2. Lay out and drill clearance holes for all screws (the screws connecting uprights **C** to top supports **A** must be high enough to clear the dado that will be cut for paper shelf **F**). Then drill countersink holes for the 1¼-inch screws in uprights **C**, making the holes just deep enough to allow the heads of the screws to be covered with putty. (The 2-inch screws holding crossbrace **D** to uprights **C** will use finishing washers, so they require no countersinking.)

Next, do a test fitting of each end assembly. When the half-lap joints fit perfectly and the top and bottom supports are exactly parallel to each other (measure at both ends), use a scratch awl through the clearance holes in uprights **C** to lay out pilot holes in top and bottom supports **A** and **B**; then drill the pilot holes.

Do a similar test assembly of crossbrace **D** and uprights **C**. Be sure that uprights **C** are parallel, then lay out and drill the pilot holes.

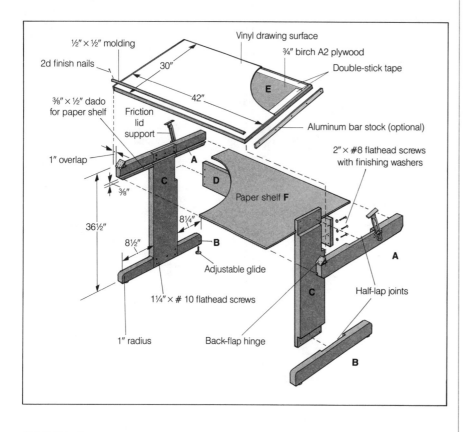

Detail: Side view

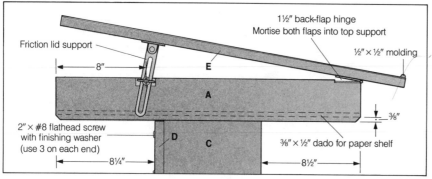

3. Glue and screw uprights **C** to top and bottom supports **A** and **B**, double-checking to make sure the supports are parallel. Using a router with a straight bit and an edge guide, cut dadoes for paper shelf **F** in assembled pieces **A** and **C** as shown. Glue and screw cross-brace **D** to uprights **C**, using the finishing washers. Install the adjustable glides on bottom supports **B**, following the manufacturer's instructions.

4. If you're using the aluminum bar stock on the sides of top **E**, install it now, using countersunk flathead screws. Be sure the heads of the screws will not hit a T-square sliding along the edge. Glue and nail the molding to the front edge of the top, using 2d finish nails. (If your lumberyard doesn't carry the right shape, make your own from a piece of ½-inch quarter round or from clear fir stock.)

Position top **E** on the frame, overlapping top supports **A** by 1 inch on each side; locate the hinge positions and screw one flap of each hinge to the underside of the top. Screw the other hinge flaps into the mortises in **A** and assemble the hinges. Next, lay out and install a friction lid support on each side of the top, following the manufacturer's instructions and the detail drawing.

5. Fill the screw holes in uprights **C** with putty. Finish-sand the frame, top, and paper shelf, removing all excess glue and putty and easing all edges except those around the upper face of the top. Apply polyurethane penetrating oil sealer to all wood parts except the upper face of the top. Slide paper shelf **F** into its dado. Finally, apply double-stick tape around the edge of the top and add the vinyl drawing surface.

BUY		TO MAKE		
Clear Douglas fir				
1	10-foot 2 by 4	2 Top supports	**A:**	1½" by 3½" by 26"
		2 Bottom supports	**B:**	1½" by 3½" by 26"
1	7-foot 2 by 10	2 Uprights	**C:**	1½" by 9¼" by 36½"
1	4-foot 1 by 10	1 Crossbrace	**D:**	¾" by 8⅞" by 40"
Birch plywood (grade A2)				
¾-inch 3- by 4-foot piece		1 Top	**E:**	¾" by 30" by 42"
Fir plywood (grade AB)				
½-inch 3- by 4-foot piece		1 Paper shelf	**F:**	½" by 26" by 37¹¹⁄₁₆"

MISCELLANEOUS
Vinyl drawing board cover, 29½" by 42" • 6 flathead Phillips woodscrews, 2" by #8, with finishing washers • 20 flathead Phillips woodscrews, 1¼" by #10 • 1 pair 1½" back-flap hinges • 2 friction lid supports • ½" by ½" fir molding sufficient to make 1 piece at 42" • ³⁄₁₆" by ¾" aluminum bar stock sufficient to make 2 pieces at 30", with flathead screws (optional) • 4 adjustable glides • 2d finish nails • Double-stick tape • Wood glue • Wood putty • Polyurethane penetrating oil sealer

Wall-Hung Shelves

Every office needs shelves, and here's a simple, wall-hung design that meets many storage needs. Our plans call for rabbet and dado joints, and inset metal shelf standards for adjustable shelves. To cut the joints, you'll need a radial-arm or table saw or a router.

To build the shelves with simpler joints, or to change the size or configuration of the shelves, see the options discussed under "Variations," below.

1. Cut all pieces to size. Rabbet sides **A** to receive fixed shelves **B**. Cut dadoes in sides **A** and divider **C** to receive the shelf standards. (Typical shelf standards are ³⁄₁₆ inch by ⅝ inch, but check the measurements of yours, then dado so the standards will be flush with the face of the boards.) Cut dadoes in fixed shelves **B** for divider **C**. Finally, notch the divider for mounting cleats **E** as shown in the drawing.

2. Cut the shelf standards to length, making sure that the position of the slots in each standard corresponds exactly; to do this, measure and cut one track, then use it as a pattern for the others. Nail the standards into their dadoes in sides **A** and divider **C**.

3. Assemble the shelves with their front edges down on a flat surface. Spread glue in the dadoes in fixed shelves **B**, then nail the shelves to divider **C**, using 6d finish nails. Next, glue and nail sides **A** to fixed shelves **B**. Spread glue for mounting cleats **E**, drop the cleats into place, and nail them to divider **C**. Then nail through fixed shelves **B** and sides **A** into **E**.

4. Finish-sand all exposed surfaces, easing all sharp edges, then apply the clear wood finish or stain of your choice.

5. To hang your shelves on the wall, drive 3-inch screws through mounting cleats **E** into studs or other solid backing in the wall. Then install shelf support clips and set shelves **D** in place.

Variations

Our simple shelves are readily adaptable to many sizes and situations. The shelves can be be built with clear pine, Douglas fir, or No. 2 Common pine. In any case, the lumber should be kiln-dried. If you'll be storing binders or large books, substitute 1 by 12 lumber for the 1 by 10s; for smaller books or shallow display shelves, use 1 by 8s.

The shelves can also be expanded in height and width. If you increase the height beyond 4 feet, add another fixed shelf. If you widen the shelves, limit each shelf span to a maximum of 32 inches to

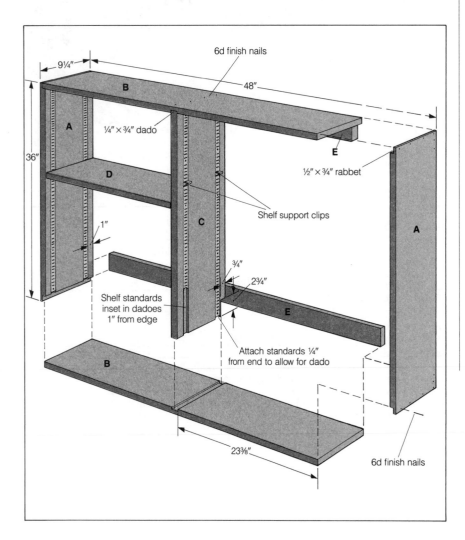

avoid sagging and add another divider if necessary.

To build the shelves using only hand tools, eliminate the rabbets and dadoes; use butt joints for all lumber connections and adjust the lengths of fixed shelves **B** and divider **C** appropriately. Mount the shelf standards on the surface (you'll need to shorten the adjustable shelves) or substitute shelf pegs that fit in holes drilled in the sides and divider.

BUY		TO MAKE		
Pine or Douglas fir (grade to suit)				
3	10-foot 1 by 10s	2 Sides	A:	¾″ by 9¼″ by 36″
		2 Fixed shelves	B:	¾″ by 9¼″ by 47½″
		1 Divider	C:	¾″ by 9¼″ by 35″
		4 Adjustable shelves	D:	¾″ by 9¼″ by 22¾″
1	8-foot 1 by 3	2 Mounting cleats	E:	¾″ by 2½″ by 46½″

MISCELLANEOUS
Slotted metal shelf standards sufficient to make 8 pieces at 34½″, with nails • 16 shelf support clips • 6d finish nails • 6 drywall screws, 3″ by #8 • Wood glue • Clear wood finish or stain

Index